ENDORSEMENTS SUCKCESS

"As a top athlete, I know how devastating fear of failure can be, both for your performance and development. With scientific facts hidden in captivating stories this unconventional book shows how to liberate yourself by embracing all possible scenarios."
—Janette Hargin, Freeskiing World Champion

"The business world hails success and punishes failure, but in our agile age succeeding sooner often boils down to failing faster. This book shows you how to get it right by getting it wrong!"
—Dr. Jonas Ridderstråle, bestselling author of Funky Business and a Global Top 30 Management Guru

"Interesting and inspiring! SUCKCESS is thinking outside the box. SUCKCESS is finding your personal leadership. SUCKCESS is achieving your goals. SUCKCESS is going beyond traditional success to find something more sustainable and infinitely more valuable. You cannot win if you do not dare to lose!"
—Franc Matjaž Zupančič, Secretary of State, Republic of Slovenia

"Can creativity and success be facilitated by accepting our shortcomings? This book provides the interesting suggestion that in fact it might."
—Simon Kyaga, Senior Consultant in Psychiatry at Karolinska Institutet, one most prestigious medical universities in the world

"It's FANTASTIC! Authentic and important thoughts and ideas in a page turning format. Wonderful!"
—Henrik Fellesson, CFO at SIWI - Stockholm International Water Institute

"Since the day we met, Joakim struck me as an original thinker, someone who weaves together social science and unique insights. This book is a fun ride through history, revealing that the way to the next level is, ironically, by embracing aspects of ourselves we most despise. In an age where nothing makes sense, this book will guide you back to your true north—and show the way forward for yourself and your business."
—Dave Logan, New York Times bestselling coauthor of *Tribal Leadership*

SUCKCESS

FREE FROM FEAR
FULL OF POWER

AHLSTRÖM & HIRASAWA

ARCHWAY
PUBLISHING

Book cover design by Andrea Norden Studio.

Archway Publishing books may be ordered through booksellers or by contacting:

Archway Publishing
1663 Liberty Drive
Bloomington, IN 47403
www.archwaypublishing.com
1 (888) 242-5904

ISBN: 978-1-4808-5272-3 (sc)
ISBN: 978-1-4808-5273-0 (e)

Library of Congress Control Number: 2017919807

Print information available on the last page.

Archway Publishing rev. date: 1/23/2018

To Hanna and Tove

CONTENTS

PREFACE

"Joakim Ahlström is an internationally recognized expert and pioneer in the field of leadership and personal development. His unique ability to harness human potential and to inspire high performance has contributed to the success of global companies such as Coca-Cola, Volvo, Ericsson and IKEA."

That's how I'm normally introduced in a business context. Nobody ever mentions the pea soup—the full bowl of pea soup that landed upside-down with a splash in my lap. It happened when I was eight years old, and the heat from the soup made me stand up. As I did, the soup ran down my brown corduroy pants and left a dark stain over my crotch. The soup was smoking hot, but the heat faded into the background as I was overwhelmed by the far more intense feeling of shame.

One year earlier, I had moved across the country with my parents and my big brother. Now we were back where I had grown up, and I spent the day in school with my old classmates. I didn't like it. Everything and everyone had changed, and I felt misplaced and insecure. I sensed the curious glances the moment I entered the classroom, and I despised being the center of attention.

Now, standing in the school canteen covered in pea soup, face shining red, I was a true spectacle. I had gotten everybody's attention. As I heard the cool kids laughing and saw the cute girls whispering, I wanted nothing more than to disappear. And so I did.

I left and didn't go back. I disappeared in a much broader sense. I decided never to put myself in a position like that again, to avoid anything with the slightest resemblance of the spotlight.

I failed. Two years later I was forced onto a stage to deliver a two-word line in a school Christmas play. My stubborn attempts to get a role behind the curtain had been in vain. I walked onto the stage in a haze and went completely blank. My short line was gone. With the spotlight in my face, I stood silently, sheepishly. Then I left. Again.

Afterward my teacher said to forget about my failure. It wasn't that bad, she said. She was wrong. It was bad. I hated myself for failing again. In my head, I repeatedly relived my version of the experience—one in which I could hear the whole audience laughing at me.

The failure made me realize I couldn't avoid the spotlight for the rest of my life. I needed a new strategy to protect myself from becoming a laughingstock again. My solution was rigorous preparation. I wrote and rehearsed manuscripts before the smallest human encounter. I noticed I had a talent for preparing smart and funny things to say and found comfort in doing so. This turned into an unconscious routine, and as a grown-up I even found myself rehearsing what to say to the cashier at the grocery store.

If I was caught off guard by somebody spontaneously starting a conversation with me, I would get tongue-tied, but apart from those rare incidents (I had become quite good at holding people at a distance), I was safe.

Ironically, as I developed quite an ability to write and to deliver thoughtful and entertaining speeches, it became part of my job. Though I almost panicked every time I was about to go on stage, my preparations prevented me from becoming a laughingstock, and though I didn't improve much, my performances were passable and I felt slightly less anxious as my experience grew. In short, life went on without any major misfortunes.

Until one day. The room was not big, but there were a lot of people in it. As usual, I had prepared for days and I knew my script word for word. I was introduced and walked onto the stage. As I did, an iron fist clutched my lungs. All air was gone. I managed to say a few words but had to stop talking to avoid hyperventilating. I pretended to need a drink of water and headed for a table with a glass and a bottle. My hands trembled as I poured the water into the glass, I started sweating heavily, and I could hear my heavy breathing. I stood panting for a long while, and the episode was excruciatingly embarrassing. Eventually I could talk again and was able to pick up a thread in my manuscript. On a very shaky footing, I finished my speech and left in shame. Again.

I prepared even more carefully, but the same thing happened again. I started opening my speeches with jokes to draw laughter, but I would lose my breath a few minutes later anyway. I did voice and breathing exercises before my speeches, but this didn't help. I tried every trick in the book but still failed.

Then I gave up. Completely drained of energy, completely out of hope, I declared myself beaten. I would remain a laughingstock for the rest of my life. *Screw this*, I told myself. *Let's be the laughingstock. Let them laugh.* To my surprise, those words brought me relief.

Instead of avoiding embarrassment, I deliberately did things that would make people laugh at me or would make me appear weird. I played around with uncomfortably long silences. I tripped on purpose and fell heavily. I spilled water on my shirt while drinking. And it was fun. I started owning the laughingstock label and accepting it within. It became my friend, and as the panic attacks disappeared so did my need for a detailed script for every speech. Instead, I could speak freely from my heart, be spontaneous, show my emotions, be super serious, and also make a complete and utter fool of myself.

With my new and genuine self on stage, I flourished as a speaker. I was relieved that I no longer had to prepare for days for a half-hour performance, but one day before speaking to a large group of business leaders in Amsterdam, I felt I wanted to do this. I wrote a script and rehearsed it a few times the evening before my talk.

I felt free on stage the next day. Sometimes I stuck to the script, and sometimes I spoke from my heart, all depending on the reactions I got from the crowd. Then, as I finished, something I had never experienced before happened. The audience rose.

For the first time in my life I got a long, thunderous standing ovation.

I had become free to move between the extremes, free to be anything from a laughingstock to the best pre-pared speaker ever and a perfect combination of both. When I gave myself access to all facets of myself on stage, I won fame and fortune, speaker awards and book deals. Above all, I gained an inner peace and a sense of well-being I had never experienced before.

* * *

"David Hirasawa is a practical thought leader who works with management, strategy, and leadership development at an international company. He has a background in political theory and philosophy, and his ability to bring stories to life has made him a highly appreciated author within the popular literature genre."

Yes, that's how I'm normally introduced, and every time it happens, I think of wellies—not wellies in general but a certain pair of wellies with worn rubber soles. I recall the twelve-year-old version of myself in those wellies, slithering around on a steep mountain wall as I hiked in the north of Sweden with my father. There was a storm and I kept slipping in the snow. I remember considering accidentally losing those wellies, dropping them down the gorge beneath us, and proceeding in my socks just to quit slipping.

The wind and the slush weren't my father's fault. Indeed the weather changes with notorious speed in the mountains, but even now the memory pisses me off.

My parents divorced when I was two years old, and the day before my dad was to pick me up for the hike, my mother reminded him that I needed new shoes. Dad disagreed, saying my old wellies would suffice. Before departing, however, he was happy to demonstrate the brand-new hiking boots he had bought for himself. He even assumed I would be impressed and happy for him.

Walking in his top-shelf boots, my dad was never more than a few steps behind me that day, but never before or since have I felt so abandoned. Feeling completely alone, I struggled through the loud, cold wind, and in the end, we made it back safe.

Growing up, I would see my father only every second weekend, and to me that was far too little. I think he felt the same way because he always made sure that our time together was packed with interesting activities. Still, on Sundays, he would often drop me off at my grandmother's house because he felt he needed to work. He would sit at the kitchen table with heaps of documents, preparing for the approaching week. Even though my father was absent eleven out of fourteen days, on that fourteenth day, he decided to be absent again, and that hurt my feelings.

On a certain level the hiking experience was the nail in the coffin for me. Returning from it, I made a solemn promise that when the time came for me to be a parent, I would never make my kids feel abandoned. Being physically or mentally absent as a parent was not okay, I decided. As a father, I would always be present.

At the age of thirty, I married.

As I was going on parental leave with our first daughter, I was close to signing a book deal with a prestigious publishing company, and I was eager to put in the extra hours needed to make my manuscript good enough. Gradually, the days with my daughter, which were supposed to be cozy and full of laughs, became nothing but a long wait for the night to arrive, the time when I could dive back into the novel I was working on.

Working until early morning at the kitchen table, I would be exhausted the day after. Going to the swings in the park with my daughter became nothing but a chore. Still, I repeated the cycle every twenty-four hours. In the daytime I was a sleepy zombie, present only in flesh. I told myself this was only temporary; I would continue on this way only until reaching some vaguely defined literary success.

Success didn't happen, though. In the end my manuscript was rejected, so my struggle continued like before.

We had a second child, and when it was time for me to go on parental leave again, I dreaded the months ahead. (Yes, this is Sweden, and we take great pride in gender equality and in our social welfare system.) At the same time, I could not accept feeling the way I did. I felt bad about myself and did everything I could to fight the feeling, but my resistance only seemed to nurture my negative sentiments.

Committed to my childhood promise not to be absent, I soldiered on, doing all in my power not to become the ungenerous and self-centered kind of father I had resented as a child. But why was this so difficult? I had envisioned myself being there for my children with lots of humor, enjoying every moment. Now I hated parenthood, and I absolutely loathed myself for hating it. I saw that my choices were the kind only dads like my own would make, and I resented myself for this. My life became a constant struggle against myself, but I saw no way out of my destructive behavioral pattern.

And so I collapsed. My wife and daughters had taken off for a mini-vacation with my in-laws, leaving me with nothing but coffee and writing. At least that's how I had imagined it, but as I stared into my laptop at the kitchen table, the room started spinning. My heartbeat became irregular and my vision blurry.

The doctor stated the obvious. I was exhausted and depressed. There was nothing to do but to rest and to see a shrink called Anders, a guy in worn-out flannel pants, woolen socks, and sandals. Still, all I could think about was time going down the drain, time that could have been spent writing. The ground beneath me was turning into quicksand. The harder I reached for success, the more I sucked as a dad, as a partner, and as a writer. Reluctantly I had become the ultimate absent father, both physically and mentally. As I saw how the burden my wife had to carry on her own grew, so did my bad conscience. We argued a lot and divorce came closer. The irony wasn't wasted on me: everything now happened exactly the way I had decided never to allow. The harder I had resisted being an absent father, the more absent I had become.

That's when I realized what I had to do. I finally gave myself permission to be completely absent. I would not just be absent mentally from sleep deprivation but would go absent full-on. During the day, I would not look after the kids at all. At night, I would only sleep.

I spent all the time I possibly could on my own. I allowed myself to enjoy the freedom of being completely self-centered, of giving nothing of myself to anyone else. I was totally ungenerous. In other words, I completely embraced the feeling I had tried so hard to run away from, and that's when things changed. It was a sudden and powerful shift. As I stopped fighting being an absent father, I got back my energy. Fully acknowledging my need to be absent also made it possible to relieve my wife by expressing my need for support to my mother and my in-laws.

I started writing for real in the daytime. I could have spent those hours with my kids—and some will still say

I should have—but I chose not to. I slept at night and wrote during the day. I replaced nocturnal espresso with daytime tea, and as I did, my writing wasn't as jittery as before. I loved writing, and after writing from ten to three, I longed for my daughters. When it was time to pick them up at their grandparents' house or at day care, I was again full of love. I hugged them and kissed them and talked with them, and I loved it. We went to the swings and laughed.

I know they noticed I was more present than before. True, I was also away more, but now when I was with them, I was really there, not sad, stuck in my own thoughts, and longing for the evening. They were no longer obstacles to my passion. The conflict was gone, and I realized they didn't mind at all that I was writing! They thrived on having a father who gave them his full attention and support when he was there. But even if they had wanted me to be around more, I needed those hours to myself. I still do, and that time away still makes me feel good. So am I an absent or a present father? Well, both—only more real, more alive, more fun.

When it comes to boots, however, or to rain gear, winter clothes, overalls, fleece pants, summer clothes, mittens, scarves, hats, beanies, sport clothes, swimming clothes, skiing clothes, dancing clothes, or soccer clothes, a part of me still can't let go. I'm meticulous about these things, and I know I'm taking aim at my father. Yes, it's about the wellies. I'm okay with my father now. I love him and I know he has always loved me, but I still recall his lack of support that day we went mountain climbing; I will not forget the sound of that brutal wind, the cracks in the glaciers, the sense of slipping, or my father trotting along in his perfect brand-new boots.

And my success as a writer? It's progressing nicely.

*   *   *

Many years before my collapse I had found a friend who was very much like me. Even when we were in our later teens and were partying and getting ourselves into trouble, we would discuss things, and it soon became obvious that we shared something at the core. We talked, we liked what the other had to say, and soon enough we started taking notes along the way, dedicated to pinning down our views for ourselves. Both of us, each from his own viewpoint and point of interest, went on to study those things. Later this became our jobs; we could go looking for incidents and examples, narrowing things down little by little one step at a time.

The world of management and leadership became our lives. This was a weird world, we thought. In a way, it was rather vague. Was it psychology? We were no psychologists. Was it philosophy? Well yes, in a way. Was it economics? Not in a direct way, although management theory most definitely has to do with money. Was it about well-being? It should be, but it wasn't, not really. We read books and threw them away. They went off the shelves into our hands, and when we had finished or half-finished one, we tried to find a better, more exact one, reflecting our vision about how management and leadership need to change.

Our experience was that theories lacked psychological insight (even when they claimed to be psychological), were deficient from a philosophical viewpoint (even when the author claimed to be something of a philosopher), shared no useful ideas about how to make more money (although money appeared to be the ultimate form of success), and did not seriously guide anyone to feeling better (even though following the theories was supposed to produce that result). The Gladwells, the Kahnemans, the Freakonomists, the Druckers, and the Tolles—we gave them all a go. Indeed, we read them with great interest, took their messages to heart, and applied their advice.

But after all that reading and applying, it dawned on us how failure has become the sworn enemy of our time. The focus is on getting up earlier, working harder, and doing more in less time, and although to some degree we sympathized with this ambition, we were getting sick of it. As for those books about being sick of it—*The Happiness Trap* and the like—we were getting sick of them too! It seemed to us that the greatest achievement of management theory was spreading the fear of failure: the harder people were pushing to break through, the bigger the fear of failure grew. The leadership and self-improvement genres thrive on people's basic fear of not being good enough, of not measuring up to high standards.

The problem, as the seven stories ahead illustrate, is that failure and success are not separate. They are interconnected and cannot exist without each other. In doing just about anything to avoid hearing that they suck, people ruin their chances of success. Furthermore, the unpleasant and embarrassing spot in their personalities, the one where they have learned that they suck, is also the spot where well-being and success begin. When we put it like this, though, the idea still sounded a bit unclear, so we decided to explain it more thoroughly in a book. To get started, we wanted to specify what the book needed to be like, and here is what we decided.

1. The book would be about this one powerful idea, which, for want of a better word, we called *suckcess*.

2. Never in the book would we ask the reader to add anything or to suppress any part of the self. Instead, we would show that who one already is offers enough.

3. To get our message across, we would rely on real-life stories. These stories had to be true. Furthermore, the seven tales we would tell needed to be page-turners good enough to make people read from start to finish, even without the didactic aspect of the stories.

4. Last but not least, we would show the reader how achievement should not and mostly will not come at the expense of well-being.

We began writing, discussing, and rewriting. We went for walks on half-hour lunch breaks that ended up lasting three hours. Had we been able to pin down the idea? Had we found a good way of presenting it, and had we reached all the way to the core of it?

We decided to publish a text on the social media networks to see what kind of response we would get. In a world where the vague and often misunderstood concept of acceptance is widespread, we thought hardly anyone would care, but we could not have been more wrong.

We were taken aback by the response. We didn't think our text about the importance of being pessimistic was extreme, but people were quite upset. One man sent us a letter so long he must have spent the better part of a day writing it. His elegant, old-fashioned handwriting had probably taken decades to master. He told us how stupid we were to encourage negative energy in a world already so full of negative energy.

The man was angry and used ugly words, but he was quite convincing. He wrote that most of his colleagues were honest people with good intentions, trying hard to improve things as they pursued agreed-upon goals. But one colleague, slouching in his chair, would never miss an opportunity to make his objections heard. Whatever solution was proposed, the letter writer said, this character would immediately be against it and would not yield to reason. People were waiting impatiently for this permanent pessimist to retire so they could do their jobs without an obstacle.

The two of us were quite put off by the letter. We were still finding our feet about this new perspective of ours. We knew we were on to something, an idea that had already helped us solve some major problems—a surprising and sometimes counterintuitive way of doing things that had helped us to achieve what we set out to do and to feel at peace with ourselves. However, we didn't have a word for it, and we were not quite sure how the concept worked. So when we published the text and got angry letters, especially that letter from the skeptic, we began to give up on the effort. We felt ashamed and embarrassed. When family members and friends asked about our book project, we said all was fine. We had been working on it for so long that we didn't have the guts to tell them the project was grinding to a halt. We convinced them that everything was headed in the right direction, that the book would soon be on the store shelves, and that we would be signing copies until our hands could no longer stand the strain.

For quite some time, however, we did nothing. Whenever we saw each other for coffee or a beer, we made sure not to mention that book idea we had had a while ago, the one that had seemed so fine at first but that now had us ill at ease. What a stupid idea it had been. Never ever would we talk about it again.

This was our silent agreement.

INTRODUCTION

"We suck!" the ancient Romans said.

The Romans were quite well organized. They would go on to build road systems, aqueducts, multi-story buildings, and many other things that required inventiveness, ambition, and determination. The Romans would conquer most parts of Europe, using meticulously developed military tactics and machinery. They were the masters of the European continent. When came to naval warfare, however, the Romans were much inferior to the Carthaginians. For the Romans, the growing Carthaginian civilization on the southern shores of the Mediterranean, in what is today Tunisia, North Africa, was becoming a problem.

The Carthaginians built their empire on trade, and ships made this trade possible. These ships became more and more advanced over time, and while the Romans were busy inventing and improving ballistae and catapults useful on land, the seafaring knowledge of the Carthaginians kept expanding. Thus, several centuries before Christ, fear spread among the Romans. The Roman senator Cato the Elder was so concerned that whenever he gave a speech, no matter the subject, he always ended it by saying, "Carthage must be destroyed!"

The Carthaginians' seafaring skill gave them a huge advantage, and it seemed just a matter of time before they gained supremacy in the Mediterranean. The Roman Empire faced a crisis, and the Roman leaders panicked. They had to do something, whatever it took, and do it fast. The Romans tried copying the ships of their rivals but failed. They tried copying their rivals' technique for navigating the seas but failed. Sources say the Romans went so far as to kidnap Carthaginian engineers, using torture to make them reveal the secrets of their naval supremacy, but again failed. The Romans were behind, and with each failed attempt to close the gap with their rivals, their despair grew. Still, the Romans blindly fought on. They failed and then failed again, and with each failure, success seemed more distant. As history reveals, however, the Romans would succeed.

The solution was a boarding device called a corvus.[1] It was a bridge of sorts with a sharp, beak-like hook underneath. The Romans would approach one of the elegant North African ships, unfold the heavy corvus over the enemy vessel, hook on to it, and from there start what was essentially a land battle, using Roman weapons and Roman tactics. The Romans would run with swords in hand, fighting in a way they knew well through experience, all thanks to their invention, the corvus.

---

[1] It's either *corvus* or *harpago*. They are practically the same thing; here, for no particular reason, we stick with corvus.

The bridge became the game-changer, but what happened before that? Well, eventually the Romans swallowed the bitter pill. Having done the same old same old—pushing, trying harder, adding more force, and failing—the Romans let go of the self-image of superiority to which they had clung so desperately. They accepted their naval weakness, and once they did, they finally started looking for new ways to approach their dilemma. "Now that we have finally accepted that we completely suck at this, let's move on to find out how we can be successful!" the Romans said.

In many respects, the Roman ships were still poor, and quite a few of them would sink as soon as the sea got rough, but with the advantage gained through the corvus, the Romans could afford these losses. Mylae, Sulci, Tyndaris, and Ecnomus all would be Roman victories, and before long, Carthage was indeed destroyed.

If we are blinded by the invention of the corvus, however, we fail to see the important paradox that brought it to life. We call this the paradox of suckcess. The corvus was a brilliant invention, but for quite some time, the prevalent perspective made that invention impossible. The Romans were obsessed with beating the Carthaginians and held on to a positive outlook despite the poor results. Change started happening only when the Romans admitted, "We suck."[2]

---

[2] Okay, you're right. The Romans did not speak English, but from time to time they sucked just the same.

"We truly suck when it comes to traditional naval warfare." Until they spoke this painful truth, the Romans were hopelessly stuck, losing every battle. But acknowledging this simple and quite obvious fact finally gave the Romans access to the world of possibility that they were so desperately trying to reach—a world where any new measure could be taken, where any new idea could be born, and where one simple invention could win a war.

To us, the corvus might seem like an obvious idea. It makes good sense. Today, however, we reject the paradox that saved the Roman Empire and instead adopt the ways that led the Romans to fail. In the modern Western world, we boost our egos and tell each other we can do the impossible if we keep doing the same thing more stubbornly. We must try harder, never give up, and look at the bright side. Wherever we go, whatever we try to achieve, someone is always around to remind us to keep smiling, to convince ourselves by convincing others, to grow our personal brands, to tend to our façades, and to fake it till we make it.

Do not get us wrong. A positive spirit is a good start on any journey as long as it doesn't prevent you from reaching the place you set out to find. But chances are that trying more forcefully will only limit your mode of action. Trying hard to be jolly all the time drastically will limit your scope, blinding you to the endless possibilities outside of that narrow spectrum. This is quite the opposite of what the Romans had to do to secure success. Forcing yourself to be cheerful when the outcome is poor is painful, dishonest, and delusional.

So what does all this mean for you?

Suckcess never was a proper word, but we made it up to label the paradox. By *suckcess* (a word that could be coined only by someone who sucks at spelling), we mean a kind of success that can be reached not only by accepting but by making use of the fact that in some respects, we do suck. By doing this, we can achieve what we desire while leaving nothing of what we are behind.

The paradox of suckcess is as old as humankind. People experience the paradox but do not have a word in their vocabularies to describe it. For many of us, the most painful failures have also brought relief with the realization that all hope was gone and all we could do was to accept failure and move on. When all seemed lost, we won something very valuable, and in that moment, we regained full access to ourselves, to the entire spectrum of our skills and capacities. Only when we finally dared to head in what we had learned to think of as the wrong direction did we become free to fully access the positive side of the spectrum.

The paradox of suckcess offers endless possibilities, and we want to share a few of them so you can find your own way to put this paradox to use. But what about the people who tell you to disregard the negative and to use affirmations to boost a positive spirit, who tell you to bang your head against the wall until you break through, all the while smiling and cheering? Well, the time has come to reach further.

Making use of seven real-life stories, we will bit by bit unveil all aspects of the paradox of suckcess. We invite you to get to know the haunted CEO who handled a crisis by accepting that he could be both a sinner and a saint; to meet the Chinese pirate queen who managed to go all the way to the finish by allowing herself to quit; to have a close encounter with the sports coach who won it all by deliberately acting the loser; to be surprised at the five-year-old kid who taught her parents about being the victim from time to time to become a hero in the end; to watch up close how becoming a genius in a woolen dress requires full-on foolishness; to learn how the rocket engineer from the space race era had to be skeptic to believe in what he was doing, and to read about the lonely teen whose wish to be a pioneer could be fulfilled only through rejection.

Considering how the paradox of suckcess has worked for the successful people and organizations we have studied and supported, not to mention all the problems it has solved for us professionally as well as in our private lives, we are quite sure you will benefit from it. Our book is about this one simple thing. We have discovered it, tested it, and refined it. Now it is time for us to share it with you.

Joakim Ahlström and David Hirasawa
Stockholm, January 22, 2018

CHAPTER 1

The Sudden Disappearance of the Haunted CEO

BECOMING A SAINT
BY EMBRACING YOUR
INNER SINNER

In a world where CEOs try to come across as saints whenever the organizations they lead have committed sins, the people working for Akio Toyoda, CEO of the Toyota Motor Company, experienced something completely different. This story is about sticky gas pedals causing fatal accidents, a Japanese boy who wanted to improve his grandmother's life, and a thousand-year-old answer that was lost on the way.

YOU COULD HAVE CUT THROUGH THE air with a knife that day. The atmosphere in the room was antagonistic, to say the least. Although the man who was the center of attention—Akio Toyoda, CEO of Toyota—had brought his closest allies, he appeared nothing less than fair game. He was the youngest man ever to occupy this position, and crouching in his chair he resembled a child who against his will had been given the leading role in the school play. He sat at the podium, waiting for his chance to give his view on what had happened.

After some technical issues with the microphone, Mr. Toyoda's lips started moving, but instead of the trembling voice of a man whose competence and judgment had been called into question, the sound of flashing cameras dominated the room. It seemed that the ruthless dynamics of the play taking place were far more powerful than Akio Toyoda.

A witch hunt had taken place in the months leading up to this day, with fingers pointed, accusations made, and blame assigned. Everyone's attention had been directed toward the huge organization led by Mr. Toyoda. In the not-so-distant past, someone had committed a sin, and now everyone wanted to hunt down the sinner. The blame game had been going on for quite some time and was getting out of control. The public wanted to see heads roll, and lawyers, politicians, and all kinds of experts were digging in the dirt. Were the accusations true, and if they were, what would the consequences be? Was Mr. Toyoda to blame for what had happened, and if he wasn't, who should be held responsible?

All over the world people were deeply upset, and no wonder. Six months earlier, a family had found itself racing to death in a car with a sticky gas pedal and malfunctioning brakes. That car, now a pile of scrap metal, had been manufactured under Mr. Toyoda's supervision. He had not been the one who assembled the car in the factory. He had not been the head of the plant, nor had he designed the car model or the brakes or the gas pedals, but he was the CEO of the Toyota Motor Company, famous worldwide for delivering safe cars. And now Toyota owners all over the globe reported that they were experiencing the same problems that had led to the fatal accident. People were shocked by news reports about the crashes. The most gripping testimony had been a desperate phone call from the father at the wheel of one of the speeding cars. All that was left of him now were his last words, printed in the newspapers:

> "We are in a [Toyota] Lexus ... our accelerator is stuck ... there is no brakes ... hold on and pray ... pray ..."

By now, many assumed that the accident would be the end of the car company so admired up until then. Indeed, this congressional hearing was the culmination of a long, exhausting process. At last the cameras stopped flashing. It was Mr. Toyoda's time to speak, and he was reaching the most important part of his testimony, the part about guilt, blame, and sin. No one knew what to expect. Here was the head of close to half a million employees, a source of great national pride. How would he defend himself? People held their breaths. Mr. Toyoda, a descendant of the founder of the company, leaned forward so that his lips almost brushed the microphone before him.

"I take full responsibility."

And that was it; the blame game was over. The story so far had been a messy one, but this was the end of it. For anyone looking to find the true sinner, Mr. Toyoda now made himself readily available. He mentioned no one else and said, "I am deeply sorry for any accidents that Toyota drivers have experienced, [and] I will do everything in my power to ensure that such a tragedy never happens again."

Please note that he did not deny the severity of the tragedy he was responsible for and that he never expected anyone else to share responsibility with him. The blame was all on him. Everyone could lay eyes on the sinner now; he was sitting there before a vast audience—white shirt, nice tie, a proper suit—and that's when a miracle happened. Right in front of everyone's eyes, Mr. Toyoda the Sinner disappeared.

Mr. Toyoda had inherited his magic powers from his great-grandfather, Sakichi Toyoda, today considered the grandfather of the Japanese industrial revolution. Sakichi Toyoda had founded Toyota and had given birth to the simple yet powerful idea that would serve as the core of the family business from then on. Sakichi's creative spark was ignited when as a young boy in the pre-industrial era he witnessed the hard work of his mother, his grandmothers, and their colleague weavers. Sakichi saw how when a thread broke, the loom would continue going anyway, causing disastrous damage to the product. The weavers had to rework the defects as best they could, wasting material and time, and would be forced to sell the damaged product at a lower price. This pained young Sakichi, who dedicated himself to making the lives of the family weavers easier. Before long he invented a device that automatically halted the loom when a broken thread was detected.

This brought a great improvement to the quality of the weave, but there was more to it than that. Now that the machinery stopped immediately, the time between the mistake and the investigation of the problem was shorter, so the source of the malfunction could be found more quickly, just as the chances of solving a crime radically improve the sooner the detective arrives. As a consequence of young Sakichi Toyoda's clear-sighted view, it became easier to spot and to fix any weak points in the production process. Sakichi soon figured that this principle would apply to any process or system, but never did he underestimate how crucial human experience and involvement were for a system to work and to improve. He was all too aware of his weaver family's know-how to make such a blunder.

As a consequence, as Sakichi Toyoda's company grew, his employees were constantly encouraged to highlight any glitch in the system. When some part of the production process was not functioning properly, instead of looking for someone to blame, the company applauded everyone in the organization who took the role of the sinner. A hundred years later, this is still how things are done. One of Toyota's workers described it like this to us:

> Right here, right now, in the part of the process that I am responsible for, something is not running as smoothly as it should. I take full responsibility for it because I know I will not be punished for it. Actually, it's quite the opposite. By doing the right thing—attracting attention to the problem, taking the blame, acting the sinner—I myself become flawless. By playing the part of the sinner, my moral stature becomes impeccable in the eyes of my colleagues and superiors. By acting the sinner, I become a saint.

Thus, when Akio Toyoda took full responsibility at the congressional hearing that day, hardly anyone within the organization was surprised or disappointed. Instead, most workers felt a sense of pride and dignity. This was their man. In a world where many CEOs seem too keen to apply double standards and to turn their backs on the people who work for them, the people working for Mr. Toyoda now knew for certain that their leader was one of them. Heard from inside the organization, Akio Toyoda's words made perfect sense. The willingness of people to take blame for their own faults and for those of others had ensured the company's progress and well-being for nearly a century. This way of thinking and acting was not only okay but expected, as it had been transmitted from generation to generation, from employee to employee. And so, on that horrible day, an entire organization stood behind Mr. Toyoda, eager to improve. The accident resulted in historic recalls of almost ten million vehicles and a record $1.2 billion settlement. During the same period, an earthquake struck Japan and severely disrupted production. Still, only seven months later, Toyota reclaimed the title of the world's largest automaker. It shouldn't have been possible, and with any normal approach, it wouldn't have been.

But it was not just in his workers' eyes that Mr. Toyoda the Sinner disappeared. On that day, that rather short, school-boyish man was globally hailed as Mr. Toyoda the Saint for presenting a wiser path. Furthermore, he elegantly illustrated that if you are dedicated, this principle can be applied on an organizational as well as an individual level. The opposite of a sinner is a saint—a person perfect in every way—and therefore many unwisely choose to deny any sin to maintain an impeccable appearance. This is merely appearance, though, and contrary to widespread assumptions, fear of becoming a sinner does not keep us from committing new sins. It does keep us from feeling well and from becoming better versions of ourselves.

Driving out that inhibiting fear requires brave leaders. It demands that they themselves can accept blame and say "I am the sinner" and move on constructively from there. Indeed, this is the way it has always been at Toyota, and the paradox of suckcess has taken the company to the top of the world.

*   *   *

One could argue that the Toyoda version of the paradox of suckcess was born not a century ago but millennia earlier. Unfortunately, when the approach came to the attention of the rest of the world, much of its power was lost in translation. In the West, *kaizen* has been translated as "continuous improvement," which is pretty close to the original meaning but not close enough. In fact, it is quite telling that while in Japan the philosophy of kaizen is highly cherished, to most non-Japanese the concept of continuous improvement represents an oppressive, never-ending hunt for ever-smaller improvements within an organization.

And so if kaizen and continuous improvement are not the same, what is the difference, and why is that difference so important? Well, to grasp the knowledge hidden to most Westerners, you must examine the etymology of the word *kaizen*. *Kaizen* is often defined as "change for the better," but if you investigate the two Chinese ideograms forming the word, you will discover a deeper meaning. The reason for this is that the Chinese kanji are symbols as well as letters, and if you interpret these symbols incorrectly, you lose the point. The early form of the first part, *kai*, is a combination of the symbol for "to whip" and the symbol for "snake-like creature," "demon," or "bearer of sin." The two symbols combined thus give us the true meaning of *kai*—"to drive out the bad."

The original ideogram for *Zen* (not to be mistaken for the *Zen* in Zen Buddhism) represents the process of sacrifice. Consequently, kaizen is the process of sacrificing the carrier of sin to make way for the saint, and this is why in old Japanese tradition, assuming the role of the sacrificial lamb—taking blame—is about the noblest deed one can perform. The tendency so common in the West—to deny one's mistakes and shortcomings, often blaming someone else—thus stands in stark contrast with the Eastern tradition in which deliberately taking blame for a collective sin is seen as a source of eternal righteousness. In fact, the more sins one acknowledges, the saintlier one becomes. Thus kaizen is a process of change for the better that can take place only after one admits to imperfection. As long as one denies one's faults and limitations, the bad will stay. Only when one acknowledges the bad, will it loosen its grip and leave room for the good.

In environments where blame is allowed to do damage, more and more energy is invested in looking good to avoid blame, and once this dynamic is created, there is no limit to how costly it can become. In oppressive environments, the tendency is to avoid blame by putting the spotlight on the person sitting next to you. That's the basic idea of the blame game, and those playing it pass blame around like a hot potato. This destructive system of mind is tightly linked to a behavior called external-ization. To externalize is to put something outside of its borders. In economics an externality is a cost that affects someone who did not choose it and who probably didn't have a say in the process. An externality would occur when the owners of an industrial plant dump waste material off-site, saddling locals with the disposal cost rather than paying it themselves.

In a more abstract sense, by making excuses, you exter-nalize the guilt associated with your actions. In Freudian psychology, externalization is the unconscious defense mechanism by which you project your internal flaws onto the outside world, primarily onto other people. To reach your goals, you must reverse the process. It might seem counterintuitive at first, but you need to accom-modate sin or blame by taking full responsibility for it, and preferably, you should take action before the blame starts jumping around from one person to the next like flees in a dormitory. If you're not okay with accepting responsibility, there will always be a battle over who the sinner is.

So does this mean that we encourage you to let others be unfair to you or to act out of line at your expense? No, that's not right. If you've been taught that it's sinful to strike back when others are mean to you, this might even be a new opening for you. By all means strike back if that's what you need to do, and don't feel bad for doing so. Your goal is to access the full set of options so that you can choose the actions that best serve your purpose and a greater good.

Putting this aspect of the paradox to use can be as simple as starting every discussion about a detected problem with a round of introspection. Encourage those who put in the most effort to share all the ways they might have contributed to the problem whether directly or indirectly. Allow no argument, comment, or especially blame to take place.

The moment you acknowledge sin it can haunt you no more. When the threat is removed, fear goes away. From this new position, chances are that you, like Mr. Toyoda, will be able to direct people's positive energy toward the task at hand. When you and the people around you stop blaming others, you automatically regain control of a process that was out of control. So here is the bottom line: you will be able to act constructively with power only when you are free to be the sinner, the saint, and everything in between. That is the paradox of suckcess.

CHAPTER 2

*The Blindingly Beautiful
Pirate Queen Who
Never Lost Her Vision*

BECOMING A FINISHER BY EMBRACING YOUR INNER QUITTER

The Chinese pirate queen Ching Shih (1775–1844) had plenty of opportunities to meet a glorious death. Born in a brothel and kidnapped by pirates, she spent most of her life constantly at war, striving to build the largest and most terrifying pirate empire the world had ever seen. So how did this woman manage to spend her old age in a beautiful house with a beautiful garden, with plenty of money in her coffers and no man her superior? Her secret was allowing herself to quit when necessary as a way of getting to the finish.

IF YOU STEP ON AN ANT HILL, WHEN YOU pull your foot out, you will see ants moving the eggs to safety in the many tunnels that run into the ground. Now imagine that you are some alien creature and that you have stumbled upon Earth and one of those large urban areas with humans living in every nook and cranny, like insects stacked on top of each other, producing fumes, lights, steam, smoke, and noise. Encountering this crazy metropolitan area would probably be quite similar to the experience you had when you explored the ant heap. These days, some cities are so big the label *city* doesn't seem fit anymore. They are so large and busy that scholars have them renamed "urban agglomerations" and "beta-plus world cities," but in a way, these are just new labels for giant human ant heaps.

The Pearl River Delta mega city on the south coast of China, with its estimated population of forty-four million, includes seven or eight cities joined by sprawl, and in the middle sits the ancient city of Guangzhou, or Canton, dating back to at least 200 BC. Canton is the place where the protagonist of this story, Ching Shih, grew up. This city used to be the only place in China where European traders were allowed. On ships loaded with desirable goods, they would make the dangerous journey to trade with Chinese officials. Captains and deckhands alike would come from faraway places like Scandinavia or the Americas to marvel at fireworks, elephants, and delicate porcelain.

Ching Shih grew up amid this chaos. Little is known with certainty about her early childhood, but she was already a prostitute when she reached adulthood. She serviced lewd, drunk, and scurvy-ridden men suffering nightmares about sea monsters they believed to be real. These men had traveled across unpredictable oceans haunted by pirates who would appear out of nowhere through storms and over hidden reefs.

Archaeologists do what they can to retrieve the facts about those olden times, digging up the dirt on the outskirts of the city, and thanks to them and other dedicated scholars not all is lost. Maps, weaponry, and stories passed on from one generation to the next are carefully assembled like pieces in a marvelous jigsaw puzzle. Making this daunting task even more difficult, many of the pieces left to be discovered are being drilled to shreds while the scholars try to do their work. The city already has plenty of metro lines, but twenty-one more are to be built in a hurry, and so the future city of Canton is quickly piling up on top of the past.

Ching Shih's survival required her to give herself up again and again to the foreign seafarers frequenting the brothel, but not all her customers were from faraway places. One who distinguished himself from the rest was the Chinese pirate master Zheng Yi. Struck by Ching Shih's extraordinary beauty, he kidnapped her. Kidnappings were a common practice among Chinese pirates, and it was not unusual for masters to rape male and female crew members alike into submission, only to adopt or marry them later on.

The vast Chinese-Vietnamese water world was populated with outlaws and opportunists. There were plenty of river mouths and jungle-covered islands to use as hideouts, and simple fishermen, armed only with knives and moonlighting as pirates to make ends meet, often attacked tradesmen. These fishermen-pirates were so poor that except for the fish they caught, they would subsist on caterpillars and ship rats.[3] Dressed in rags, they would make surprise attacks on heavily loaded cargo ships, quickly returning to fishing after these forays. They would strike haphazardly, making use of sudden opportunity and changes in winds, and so Chinese officials had a hard time telling the difference between pirates and honest fishermen.

Because of Vietnam's rivalry with China, Vietnamese rulers offered Chinese pirates a permanent haven on the Vietnamese coast to encourage attacks on Chinese vessels, and when these ragtag bands were united under

---

[3] We must say these facts surprise us. Weren't there plenty of fish in the sea? Or maybe caterpillars and rats are way more delicious than one would expect. For further reading, see D. H. Murray's *Pirates of the South China Coast*, especially pages 78–9.

a common leader with a common set of rules the situation changed even more dramatically.

Ching Shih was of a different breed. When Zheng Yi demanded that his wife submit to any desire of his, she responded by demanding half of his fortune, half of his fleet, and half of his power. Zheng Yi was either a radical feminist far ahead of his time, or he was out of his wits in love, because he accepted all of Ching Shih's demands. When he died—some say in a storm, some say by assassination carried out on Ching Shih's orders—Shih was already a full-fledged pirate leader. To hold on to her new powers, she married her husband's former lover and right-hand man, the young Cheng Pao. With this new husband by her side, Ching Shih went to work, establishing a brand-new code of piracy. The former brothel worker banned rape and polygamy and even punished sex outside of marriage. Furthermore, unless they could be turned into wives, any women captured were to be released immediately after combat. A shrewd businesswoman, Ching Shih created an efficient network of associates on land, and loyal trading partners were never to be attacked again. Instead, to build trust and devotion, they would be paid above-market prices.

To top things off, Ching Shih's new code of piracy demanded that any bounty be immediately presented to the captain, every single penny of it, and when all was accounted for, only a slight share was returned to the pirate who grabbed it. This new surplus built a fund that financed the expansion of the fleet. With as many as eighteen hundred ships manned by eighty thousand pirates and still growing, Ching Shih was on her way to create the greatest pirate empire of all time, and she ran her enterprise with an iron fist. If she had been able to connect to our times she would have sensed the excitement of historians as they described her star rising. There had been plenty of legendary pirates before Ching Shih—Störtebeker, Henry Morgan, Black Bart, and Jean Fleury, to name only a few—and with enormous determination and discipline she was about to surpass them all.

The Chinese, the British, and the Portuguese feared the raw power of Ching Shih and her pirates' ruthless attacks. They would swim in darkness to climb an enemy vessel or set fire to their own boats and send them into an enemy fleet. After the brutal attacks were done, captives were nailed to the ship deck and beaten until they vomited blood, and when they could not vomit anymore they were gutted and fed to the fishes. Ching Shih built a fleet so superior that her pirates started to engage in eccentric behavior. Dressed up in frocks, gowns, and pearls from looted ships, they would sometimes remain seated on deck, playing, drinking, and laughing with weapons in their hands, not even pausing from their board games when confronting enemy ships. One pirate captain who was fond of stories turned his ship into a giant floating library. Enjoying their pipes, pirates would sit on top of coffers packed with gunpowder, and it wasn't until quite a few ships had caught fire or had exploded that they decided that wetting down the decks had to be part of their daily routine.

For the people on land, piracy's rise under Ching Shih's leadership certainly had its downside. They were getting fed up with being robbed, and officials received the funds to properly equip themselves for battle. But Ching Shih was now the queen of the seas. She had fought her way through life, and the men who had taken advantage of her as a young woman were now suffering from her rage. Chinese officials went so far as to ask the Europeans for help, but their humbling initiatives were to no avail. The pirates were going berserk. With riches, guns, power, and pumped-up self-esteem, they could now do anything they had ever dreamed of. Gone were the days of hiding and starving. The waters, the reefs, the islands, the coasts—all was theirs to take now. There was no force strong enough to stop Ching Shih, and she could expand her empire forever. But then, her status as the greatest pirate leader of all time within reach, she suddenly decided to quit piracy forever.

The move seemed to take everyone by surprise. In full control of the South China Sea, Ching Shih walked unarmed into the city where as a kid she'd had to give herself up as a prostitute to anyone demanding her services. After that she had given herself up to the man who had kidnapped her. Then, for many years, she had given herself up to the violent ways required of a pirate leader. In doing so, she had gained more power than anyone would ever have thought possible. Now she decided it was once again time to give up and quit fighting, so she surrendered to Chinese officials in Canton. Quitting had become her way of moving toward her goal, but it turned out that her goal was not what people around her had assumed it to be. And so, when Ching Shih decided the time was ripe, she told her crews that piracy was over.

Many of her men were unwilling to bow down under any circumstance. They were not appeased even when desperate Chinese officials offered to let Ching Shih and her pirates keep everything they had stolen as long as they quit. The worst part of a surrender was kneeling before officials to whom they felt superior in exchange for an amnesty they saw as unnecessary. Though their revered leader had done so, many of the pirates refused to follow. Surrendering to a defeated foe was shameful, but soon most of them would pay the ultimate price for not doing so. Ching Shih had reason to continue on her path of vengeance, but the pirate queen no longer seemed to hold feelings of any kind for her adversaries— neither love, hatred, fear, or a desire to conquer. She was now completely free from the grip of her former masters and thus had access to the entire palette of choices. She chose to kneel before the authorities because this served her purposes.

Ching Shih, known for her doggedness, quit piracy to try a different life. She wanted to live peacefully in a big house with a beautiful garden in Canton, no man her superior and no one bothering her again. People had begged her to go on fighting, essentially saying, "Don't you understand? This is who you are!" But Ching Shih was powerful enough to decide for herself, and she took the opportunity to live the way she desired. Drinking, gambling, and reminiscing with grandchildren on her lap, she reached the age of sixty-nine at a time when life expectancy in her part of the world was well below thirty.

*   *   *

From a distance, quitting at will may not seem remarkable. When you are caught up in the dilemma, however, choosing to quit isn't always easy, and a voice in your head or someone whose opinion you care about has probably said, "But things are going so well! You can't quit now!"

"You can't quit." That line seems innocent and well-intended at first glance, but aren't those the most constraining words ever uttered? Because you once decided to do something and proved good at it, you're now supposed to keep doing it for the rest of your life? Whenever someone says, "You can't quit," an alarm should go off in your head because this person would trap you, using your achievements to constrain your future actions. Instead of respecting your right to decide for yourself what success means, this person would have you pursue success as he or she defines it. Convention holds that you quit only when you've failed at something. Thus quitting isn't for successful people. A refusal to quit—which often means fighting to the bitter end—appeals to the weaker part of the ego, to pride and vanity.

It might appear as if we are trying to persuade you to quit, but we're not. All we ask is that you do not let fear of being labeled a quitter influence what you do with the opportunities that are yours alone. If you haven't done so already, give this strategy a try and see what happens. Chances are that when the inhibiting anxiety you've felt about being perceived as a quitter is gone, you will access the courage and joy to pursue the things you decide are important in life.

Read between the lines, the story of Ching Shih tells us that although quitting and finishing might appear to be opposites, they are interconnected, and that if you are too strongly tied to the one you will lose access to the other. When you feel free to quit what is no longer in your best interests, you gain power, and this is the liberating dynamic that we refer to as the paradox of suckcess.

In a discussion about refusing to give up and hanging on to the bitter end, the word *integrity* comes to mind. If you ask people on the street, they will probably tell you that integrity is about keeping one's word and doing what one set out to do no matter what happens along the way. This requires grit, and grit can be a good thing, but blindly sticking to a plan and plowing on regardless of any change in circumstances has more to do with insanity than with integrity.

The view that integrity is about soldiering on is also incorrect from a strictly linguistic perspective. The root of the word is *integer*, the mathematical term for a full number as opposed to a fraction, and the dictionary says integrity is about being honest, complete, and whole. If you feel it is paramount that you stick to your word no matter what happens along the way, you may be less than whole. You've proven to yourself and to everyone around you that you possess stamina and grit, but in doing so you have limited yourself to a fraction of available opportunities and have become vulnerable, weak, and unable to adapt. In addition, you have become hard to rely on, because people know that if a change of plans becomes necessary, you won't take adequate action; your loyalty is with the past, not with the present.

Integrity is not about refusing to change your mind but about allowing yourself and the people around you to choose from the whole range of options. It also means informing anyone who might be affected by a change in your plans. If you find yourself obsessively struggling to finish what you've started only because you started something to begin with, challenge yourself to give up, and while you're at it, ask yourself what you are trying to prove. What is it that you can't have others thinking about you? That you haven't got the willpower? That you're weak? Well, we are all weak at times, and our ability to embrace and to handle our weaknesses makes all the difference. When you stop resisting being labeled a quitter, you get the chance to reconnect with what you truly want and can reapply your will to your most important doings.

If we haven't convinced you yet, you might find it interesting to learn that science is firmly on the side of our paradoxical approach to quitting and finishing. One study found that teenagers who are unable to disengage themselves from trying to attain hard-to-reach goals showed increased levels of an inflammatory protein linked to diabetes, heart disease, and early aging.[4] This doesn't indicate that persistence is a bad thing but that too much of it could pose a serious threat to your health. The study also found that people who didn't stigmatize moving freely between projects—quitting one to engage in another—in general gained a greater sense of mastery.

If you want to practice your quitting skills and to avoid having only the same old stuff on your to-do list, you should start using a quit list as well.

The past is known; the future is not. Hence it is easier to calculate the cost of an investment made than to predict how much we could gain by quitting. Economists refer to what has already been spent on a project as "sunk cost," and most of us have a strong inclination

---

[4] The research report "You've Gotta Know When to Fold 'Em: Goal Disengagement and Systemic Inflammation in Adolescence" by Gregory Miller and Carsten Wrosch was published in *Psychological Science* in 2007. In a slightly less scientific experiment, Steven D. Levitt and Stephen J. Dubner set out to explore whether quitting makes people happier or unhappier. They convinced their guinea pigs to leave a major life decision to chance. Each one entered the decision he or she was facing on a website and then flipped a coin. The researchers checked back later to find out whether participants felt better or worse. It turned out that many decisions didn't affect people's happiness at all, some decisions, especially those resulting in doing something out of the ordinary (signing up for a marathon or asking for a raise) had made people less happy. Quitting made people significantly happier when it involved fundamental decisions like breaking up with a partner or leaving a job.

to believe that once we have invested something (emotion, time, money, prestige) in an endeavor, it would be a much greater loss to quit than to continue investing. The concept of sunk cost, however, exists to make this fallacy apparent and to help us see that the cost can't be recovered. In fact, no action can be undone. At every moment, there are only future choices. The pirate queen Ching Shih knew this. Her vision was not distorted by the past. As she fully embraced the possibility of quitting, she could clearly see and evaluate the potential of any path she chose.

CHAPTER 3

The Unshakable Sports Coach Who Broke the Ice

BECOMING A WINNER
BY EMBRACING YOUR
INNER LOSER

In this chapter a twenty-eight-year-old Joakim Ahlström, sitting in a bar, learns how legendary hockey coach Herb Brooks messed up the Russians. Making sure his inexperienced team would feel like a bunch of losers, Brooks managed to secure the ultimate win. He did not rely on miracles or luck, but the public still refers to the man's legendary achievement as the Miracle on Ice.

"HEY GEORGIE, YOU PACKIN'?"

I was so deep in thought that a few seconds passed before I realized what had just been said. I looked over my shoulder to see whom the hoarse voice belonged to. When I did I saw two old men, big grins on their faces, holding each other's shoulders as if they had just finished hugging but didn't want to let go entirely. They didn't look alike, but age wise they could have been father and son, the older one probably close to ninety.

The question had apparently been a jest or an inside joke, but for some reason a small revolver of the kind that old Italian mobsters carry wouldn't have seemed completely out of place. I was sitting in a shabby little Italian joint, and both men would have made great extras in the *Sopranos* television series. They had neatly cut gray hair that was thick for men their age. Both wore slacks with drain-pipe pant legs that barely touched their newly shined shoes; their short sleeves were many times wider than their thin arms, but the shirts struggled to reach around their bellies.

This wasn't Little Italy in the Big Apple, though. I was stuck on the outskirts of the Mini-Apple,[5] and I sure felt small too. I had just left a terrible sales meeting at the headquarters of a pacemaker company, and I felt like a complete loser. I had arrived there so sure of myself, convinced I'd win the deal. Now I couldn't stop thinking about my lousy performance. As soon as the discussions had gravitated toward the areas where I knew my competitor to be strong, I had panicked and started rambling incoherently. Where the hell had my prepared counterarguments gone when I needed them most?

Sitting at the bar, I wondered if the people I had met were as unhappy about the meeting as I was. I hoped not, but I had a nagging feeling I would never hear from them again. All I wanted was to go home, but my flight wasn't till the morning. Come to think of it, I didn't want to go home. I'd have to let my colleagues know we'd lost the deal. They'd probably expect an explanation, and I didn't relish the prospect of sharing how the meeting had played out. I would have to make something up.

The sight of the old men had unexpectedly distracted me from my self-loathing. I noticed the time and went to the bar to get another beer and whiskey before happy hour was over. The bartender was absorbed in a hockey game playing out on the TV behind the counter, and I stood silently until he noted my presence. When I returned to the table the two old men were sitting there.

---

[5] That's what some residents like to call Minneapolis to indicate a similarity—mostly imagined—to New York City.

From a shorter distance, I saw that only the younger man had Italian features. The other one, the one I assumed was named George,[6] looked more like an Eastern European to me. My chair was still empty and I moved it to create space between us before sitting down.

"Do you believe in miracles, son?" the Italian-looking guy asked. My hopeless facial expression had apparently given me away. I gave him an awkward smile, and as our eyes met I knew I was trapped. I saw the unwanted advice of a nostalgic old man coming my way. "Well, neither do I," he continued with a smile. "But my old friend Georgie here has taught me that the place you are in right now isn't as bad for you as you think. Come on. Tell him, Georgie!" he said, encouraging his friend.

"You tell it," George replied evasively, looking apologetically at me.

"Well then don't mind if I do," the man said, taking a deep breath as if preparing to launch, completely disregarding the discomfort of his listeners. "You see, Georgie here has been involved in creating what people wrongly consider a miracle."

I realized there was no stopping this guy. At the same time, my only other company was the voice in my head

---

[6] I later did some googling and got a hit on a Dr. Visvaldis George Nagobads (born November 18, 1921), a physician known for his role as the doctor for the 1980 US hockey team that won the gold medal at Lake Placid.

constantly badmouthing me, so I decided to give him my full attention.

"Heard of ice hockey coach Herb Brooks? The one who led a bunch of college players to victory in the 1980 Winter Olympics?" I vaguely recalled a movie with Kurt Russell I had seen some years earlier and nodded. "Good. Twenty-five years ago, almost to this day, I think, he took a bunch of boys to the same mental state that you are in now. Maybe an even worse place, but hey, who's comparing? A couple of weeks later he was hailed as a miracle-maker, but if you ask Georgie here, who got to see his magic from the inside, there was nothing supernatural to him. All he had was a unique approach to winning. Too bad the true beauty of it isn't known to the world. If it was, I wouldn't have to tell you to stop fighting the feelings you feel right now and encourage you to familiarize yourself some more with them instead."

Was this guy making fun of me? It didn't seem that way, but his remark annoyed me just the same. Familiarize? I hated feeling like this! I would have done anything to make it stop. I couldn't forgive myself for behaving like such a loser earlier that day. I'd crossed the damn Atlantic to take part in that meeting, and that's what I told him. From the corner of my eye I saw George smiling emphatically at me as if he knew all too well how I felt. "You've been taught to feel the way you do, son," he said. "You've been taught to feel like that by people who themselves have learned to hate losing. It's a vicious cycle really, a vicious cycle preventing you from performing at the top of your ability when you really need to."

"Nice to see you get going, Georgie," his friend said with a smile. "Are you going to tell the rest of the story as well, or do you want me to continue?"

"I'll tell it," replied George, suddenly energized. "I'll tell you how Coach Brooks made it possible for those boys to win that gold."

This guy got my attention immediately. His energy was contagious, and I felt he wasn't going to give me the standard pep talk, which had never had any effect on me. This was something different, and I was curious to find out what. I took a sip of whiskey and showed him I was all ears.

"You know, the last thing that crazy Coach Brooks did before the Olympics was to have his team slaughtered by the Russians in an exhibition game. He even persuaded a lot of people to make the game happen. The Russians couldn't lose; everyone knew that, and everyone wanted to see a morale-boosting victory before the Olympic tournament. Brooks thought differently. He made sure that this mentally crucial game was against the team that practically owned the gold medals in those days. They had won the gold in the four previous Winter Olympics. They had the big five—Fetisov, Larionov, Kasatonov, Makarov, and Krutov. We had a bunch of teenage college players." I smiled.

"People thought Coach Brooks had gone crazy. The tournament would be over before it even started. It was suicide. If there had been a good alternative to replace him with, I think the US Olympic Committee would have fired him on the spot, but Brooks stood his ground. After the first period of that exhibition game in the Garden, I thought I would sink into the stands. We were trailing 0–4 and our boys were already deflated. When Mike—Mike Eruzione, our captain—scored in the second it only made the Russians mad, and they buckled down to score thrice in three minutes. Their passing was flawless; they didn't miss a tackle; they were superior in every aspect. Not to mention their skating! They were beasts skating like ice princesses. This one guy, Maltsev, even did a backward-spinning pirouette, scoring their fifth." This old man had me laughing now.

"People in the stands couldn't believe their eyes! At first, they were frustrated, but after a while they just gave in and started enjoying the show. Afterwards, though, people were furious with Brooks. They said a trouncing like that, losing ten goals to three, would demoralize our young team, but Brooks didn't even try to argue with them. I just remember what he said when we left the Garden a few hours later. 'Now we're exactly where we want to be,' he said! Sounds weird? Well, it was!"

I was surprised not so much by the story but at the energy of this old man. My negative thoughts were giving way, at least for the moment.

"If you think that was weird, wait till you here what he did against the Chicken Swedes![7] You're not Swedish by the way, are you?" I didn't know what to say and just smiled sheepishly at him. I don't know what my expression told him, but whatever it was it didn't stop him.

"It was the first game of the actual tournament. Always crucial those ones. We were trailing from the start. Some Sven character scored early, and when we equaled the score some other Sven scored. With about forty seconds left in the game, the score was still 1–2 and we were losing. You know what Brooks did then?" By now the two men were bursting with excitement. Chuckling, they looked at each other, making me think of my late grandma, who could never finish a funny story because she would always burst into laughter before she got to the punchline. "He sent in the Coneheads! That's what he did. The Coneheads! With seconds left! Against their strongest defense!" This was evidently the funniest thing since Charlie Chaplin. I didn't get the point and apparently it showed.

"You see," the Italian-looking guy explained, "everyone was expecting Eruzione and his line. The first line. They were the stars, the ones who were supposed to handle situations like these. I think even the Coneheads themselves were surprised. The three of them were so used to being spectators when Brooks worked on the power plays during training that people thought they were no

---

[7] Later I found out that Chicken Swedes was a term used to describe any European players who were so disciplined that it was almost impossible to provoke them into a fight.

more vital to the proceedings than the orange cones set up during practice. No one but Brooks saw the beauty in putting the Coneheads on the ice in a situation like that. I mean, all due respect to the Coneheads, but in a way, it felt like accepting the loss. But we didn't lose, you know. Free from heavy expectations on their shoulders, they came through for us and tied the game at 2–2 with less than half a minute left! Good thing for Brooks they did. I think people would have killed him for pulling a stunt like that otherwise."

The older guy regained the baton and enthusiastically continued the story. "From then on, it felt like we just cruised through to the final round. We hammered Czechoslovakia and Norway, walked over Romania, and won easily over West Germany before the semi-final against Russia. Obviously, they were the toughest opponents possible, but to be honest, I was starting to believe in victory."

"Wait a minute," I objected. "They had just beaten you guys 10–3. How could you even think you'd stand a chance? That's an afterthought!"

"Just telling you the way I felt, son," the old man replied calmly. "I'm not saying I knew we'd beat the Russians, but I did know that having lost that big to them nine days before, our players would have nothing to lose and all to win. I also knew that state of mind would improve our chances of winning big time. And as you know, we did. Indeed, the Miracle on Ice is how it went down in the history books. Calling it a miracle, though, devalues Coach Brooks's great insight into human psychology—his innovative efforts to mentally prepare our boys and to keep their opponents unprepared for that game. Thanks to Coach Brooks, our players couldn't be any worse losers than they already were, and that's why the game appeared an inspiring opportunity to them. Their fear of losing was gone.

"For the Russian players, on the other hand, victory was the only acceptable outcome, their duty. When it came to technical skills, the Russian players were in a league of their own, but when it came to accepting loss, they were untrained and without experience. The longer the game went on without the Russians scoring a great number of goals, the more constrained they became. Our players were free and inspired right from the start. They wanted to win just as much as anyone else, and without fear of losing they could be as creative and inventive as they needed to be." He took a sip of his drink and allowed his words to sink in.

"After the victory against the Russians, though, we still needed to defeat the Finns in the final, and although Finland was a much weaker team, this was the game that worried me. After their triumph, obviously, our players were hailed as winners. This was the Cold War and they warmed the hearts of an entire nation. People were so proud and so were our boys. I saw how they enjoyed that sweet taste of victory. They loved being the winners, but I also realized they had to let go of that mental state to win the gold. Brooks, of course, saw this too. The day after the victory, he was downright mean.

He pushed the boys through the toughest physical practice ever, and the sweet taste of victory was replaced with puke. He turned that winners' train around and let everyone off at loser station."

The old man seemed done talking, but he saw me waiting for the rest of the story, so he added the obvious ending. "The final game?" He shook his head and smiled the happiest smile at the clinking ice in his glass. "I'm telling you. The poor Finnish team. They never stood a chance."

I don't remember much more of that evening. I had too much to drink. I woke up early the next morning in my hotel bed. The old man's words echoed in my head: loser station. Surely I had arrived. I had refused to admit it the day before. Now, lying in bed, staring at the ceiling, I let go of the words I had tried so hard to suppress. "I lost! That deal is lost and I'm the loser!" To my big surprise, saying this felt good. I even started laughing. This time there was no self-loathing, just acknowledgment of what had happened and of the role I had played in it. Embracing the loser within, I also realized that loser station wasn't such a bad place to be. I decided I should return there whenever I felt the need, gathering my courage not by visualizing great victories, as the average mental coach on TV would prescribe, but by getting comfortable with losing as a possible outcome.

Yes, that was it, loser station. Thanks to those two old men, I could come and go there as I pleased, but for now, I decided to stay a while. I could finally relive the excruciatingly awkward meeting in my mind to see what

I should have done differently. Back home, I would tell my colleagues all about it to get their honest feedback and advice. When I was done I stepped out of bed, took a cold mini-apple juice from the mini bar, and drank it in long, satisfying gulps.

*   *   *

The Russians couldn't lose. That was the feeling everyone—the 11,243 people in the stands, the American players, the Russian players—had after the exhibition game in Madison Square Garden that February afternoon, only a few days before the start of the Olympic ice hockey tournament. Had there been a grain of hope for the Americans before the game, it was definitely gone afterward. The swiftness, precision, and ruthlessness of the Russian hockey machine was well known, and the outcome of the game was nothing less than expected. In the five months leading up to the 1980 Winter Olympics, Team USA had played sixty-one exhibition games. The Americans had won a lot of them and that had boosted morale, but Coach Brooks had made sure that the last exhibition game before the tournament was against the Russians, the team that could not be beaten.

Brooks knew that continuously affirming positive visions, trying to fool themselves into believing they were stronger than they were, would make his players fragile. He knew that all air pumped into the balloon would escape at the smallest proof that the adversary was stronger. He knew this was so, both for his team and for its rivals. That's why his counterintuitive strategy was to make his players more okay with being losers even as they retained their passion for winning, all the while making the Russians even more unaccustomed to the concept of losing.

On February 22, 1980, only nine days after that exhibition game, Team USA was facing the Russians again, and this time the game was about a spot in the Olympic final. Brooks had set this up as a game between a team that could not, was not allowed to, and didn't know how to lose and a team unafraid of doing so. Before the game Brooks encouraged his players to cherish the moment, and of course they did! Free of fear they unleashed all their young talent, and in the first period they scored twice, just like their undefeatable opponents. Thirty minutes later, with the score at 3–3, the Russians had already started losing.

As the unimaginable and forbidden outcome became a distant possibility, the Russians were overwhelmed by fear. Three decades later Alexei Kasatonov, the Russian team's top scorer, described his feelings. "We almost panicked ... The pressure on us was almost unbearable ... We didn't know what would happen when we'd come back, what punishment we would face ... We figured we probably wouldn't be sent to Siberian labor camps, but on the other hand nobody had any idea on how they'd treat us."[8]

---

[8] "The Miracle on Ice," *The Sporting Witness* (podcast), *BBC World Service*.

You might think that fighting as if your life depends on it, the way Russian players did as fear of losing grew, increases your chances of winning. Most of the time it doesn't. Fear triggers the release of adrenaline into your bloodstream, expanding the air passages in your lungs and helping redistribute oxygenated blood to your muscles. As a result, you become a better fighter for a few minutes. If you are fighting for your life this could be a lifesaver. But in a fight that lasts more than a couple of minutes and requires more than physical strength, it's a killer. If the fight continues after the adrenaline boost has worn off, your mental and physical abilities will be severely limited, and soon your brain will start telling you that your best option for survival is to play dead. If you have ever been forced into a fistfight, you know the feeling—hands trembling and knees shaking afterward, followed by the urgent need to sit or lie down to regain your strength.

In contrast with Kasatonov, American captain Mike Eruzione offered this analysis of what happened when the score was tied and only ten minutes remained in the game: "I think the game came into our hand ... it became a game of emotions ... it became a game of conditioning."[9] The Russians suddenly were confronted with an emotion they couldn't handle, a fear they refused to acknowledge, and so they fought it. They started a fight no one can win, because fighting an emotion only fuels it. The only way to become free of an emotion is to allow

---

[9] *Of Miracles and Men.* Directed by Jonathan Hock. *ESPN*, February 8, 2015.

it to pass through you without resisting it. The more the Russians fought their fear of losing, the likelier they became to lose. The Americans, who knew the bitter taste of defeat as well as the sweet taste of victory, were accustomed to the full spectrum of emotions. For them, emotions never came into play. For them, the game was still about ice hockey, and as their opponents engaged in a different fight, the Americans claimed the victory when Eruzione scored the winning goal.

More often than we like to admit, the ability to handle emotions and to cope with anxiety or pressure plays a more decisive role in business and sports competition than technical skills and know-how. A model explaining the relationship between anxiety and performance is the inverted-U hypothesis, first presented by the Canadian psychologist Donald Hebb in 1955.[10] This hypothesis says that every team or individual has an optimal level of anxiety—or arousal, a more accurate term to describe positive stress—at which performance levels peak.

As arousal increases, so do achievements, but at a certain point arousal turns into increasing anxiety, and when it does, the output of the performer's efforts decreases. The journey leading to the top performance, the peak of an inverted *U*, is fueled by the possibility of performing well or winning. If possibility turns into anxiety, most often driven by negative thoughts about losing, the move from the pinnacle down the slope of the

---

[10] Hebb's scientific article "Drives and the CNS (Conceptual Nervous System)" was published in *Psychological Review*.

inverted *U* begins and the quality of the performance deteriorates. This increases the risk of losing, which in turn raises anxiety even more, leading the performer further away from the optimum. The decline then continues even more quickly.

In 1986 Norwegian sports psychologist Willi Railo said we can be winners only to the extent that we can be losers.[11] Railo stressed the importance of working with our "lower limit," the worst performance we can accept from ourselves. With a high lower limit, we often achieve worse results than we can accept, and that might breed negative feelings about ourselves or even allow self-hatred to thrive. To raise the roof, Railo said, we must lower the floor. Simply put, that means becoming friends with your inner loser, accepting that you, like everyone else, inevitably is a loser at times and that this is okay. If you don't, the interval between your lower and upper limits remains small, and your freedom to live, perform, and grow is restricted. Fully embracing the paradox of suckcess completely removes the lower limit, the anxiety that would inhibit your performance, and when that happens you are free to accomplish things you didn't think possible. Your zone of optimal achievements becomes a safe place where you can stay for as long as you want.

---

[11] In 1986 Railo wrote a popular book called *Best When It Counts*. He also worked as a consultant for Swedish football manager Sven-Göran Eriksson, once the manager of the English national team and the first manager to win league-and-cup doubles in three countries.

The state of having nothing to lose and all to win is sometimes called being antifragile, a concept coined and developed by Professor Nassim Nicholas Taleb.[12] The term refers to systems that increase in capability as a result of random unforeseen events, volatility, or mistakes. If there was a lottery that allowed you to win big but to get your money back if you didn't, entering it would put you in a state of antifragility.

That was the state the Coneheads entered as Coach Brooks put them on the ice, their team trailing 1–2 with forty-one seconds left in the first game in the Olympic tournament. The Coneheads—Mark Pavelich, John Harrington, and Buzz Schneider—were talented hockey players, but at that moment their strength came from the fact that no one expected them to turn the game around. With nothing to lose, they were able to unleash all their creativity and to surprise even themselves. Nobody knows for sure, but many claim that if the Coneheads hadn't scored against Sweden, Team USA would never have gotten the chance to play against the Russians.

The morning after their triumph against the Russians, Coach Brooks greeted his players with a baseball bat. A final against Finland awaited, and if his players were to have a shot at the gold, Brooks knew he couldn't put

---

[12] This Lebanese-American is without doubt one of the sharpest tools in the shed. According to *The Sunday Times*, his theories and books (*The Black Swan* and *Antifragile*, for example) on probability and uncertainty are among the most influential since World War II.

a group of satisfied winners on the ice. With strenuous exercises he took them back to the loser station again, and that made his players hungry for another victory.

But what about luck and coincidence? Maybe the stars were perfectly aligned in favor of Brooks and his team that special evening; maybe the ice happened to be irregular and bumpy in just the right way; maybe Krutov had a serious quarrel with his girlfriend that morning; maybe changes in the tide made the air conditioning in Larionov's hotel bathroom go bananas, preventing him from sleeping at all the night before the game. These are just a few of the unlimited number of imaginable reasons Brooks's team was victorious, a feat so hard to believe it was called the Miracle on Ice. If you want to continue calling it a miracle, by all means do, but please note the following facts.

After the marvelous triumph of 1980, Brooks was followed by coaches taking a more conventional approach. The next Winter Olympics took place in Sarajevo in 1984, and after only twenty-seven seconds the American team, the reigning champions, had allowed its first goal. Carrying a heavy load on their shoulders throughout the tournament, the Americans finished seventh. Team USA did not even reach the podium in any of the five Olympics after 1980. The Americans would not triumph again until 2002 when Brooks, with his paradoxical approach, came out of retirement to lead Team USA in the Winter Olympics in Salt Lake City. Once more, his team beat the Russians, eventually winning the silver medal.

CHAPTER 4

The Freewheeling Kid Who Stood Her Ground

BECOMING A HERO
BY EMBRACING YOUR
INNER VICTIM

Grown-ups lie a lot to children, all the while demanding that children always speak the truth. This is what the real-life protagonist and victim of this story, Michael, learned from his daughter. Aided by his five-year-old, Michael learned how to embrace the moments when he had no control, accepting powerlessness, even sharing his burdens. In the end, all it took for Michael and his daughter to feel good again was sitting down to tie a pair of shoes.

EASTER WAS APPROACHING AND MICHAEL and his wife had secretly bought their older daughter, Sara, her first bike. Most of her friends already had bikes and knew how to ride them. Michael did not want his daughter to be left out and was keen to help her learn. Ever since the purchase Michael and his wife had gleefully pictured how happy Sara would be. The night before Easter Sunday, they set the alarm clock for an early hour.

In the morning, as their newly awake daughter approached the living room where the shiny new bike stood with a purple bow on the handlebar, Michael was ready with his camera. "Happy Easter, darling! Look what we have bought for you! Your first bike! Isn't it nice?" Michael's wife gave up a cheer as their five-year-old entered the room.

What happened next was a complete mystery to Michael and his wife. Their daughter looked at the bike, smiled halfheartedly, and dutifully gave her parents thank-you hugs before asking what was for breakfast. And not just that: ten minutes later, for no apparent reason, she started crying quietly over her bowl of cereal.

Michael sighed deeply. It wasn't the first time something like this had happened. "What's wrong?" he asked, trying hard to hide his irritation. He got no answer.

"Why are you sad?" his wife asked, trying another approach. They had to wait a while before receiving an answer of any kind.

"I don't know," Sara offered. "Can I go to my room, please?" She rose without waiting for their permission. In the hallway, she passed her younger sister, who'd just woken up and was on her way to the breakfast table.

"Why is she crying?" asked the little one, her hair characteristically in a complete mess.

"Probably just tired. What do you want to eat?" Michael answered, changing the topic.

Michael loved his daughters, more so than most fathers, he liked to think, though he knew he wasn't the only father to believe that. But Michael had another thought he wasn't completely comfortable with and had decided to keep to himself: he suspected that he loved his older daughter a tiny bit more than her sister. They had always had a special bond, and he had a talent for perking her up when she closed down, as he and his wife referred to her emotional dips, and withdrew into herself.

"I would have wanted a pink instead of a blue one," Sara said, facing away from Michael, who had been sitting on her bedside stroking her back for several minutes. Michael disliked her being so stereotypically fragile and sensitive, and yes, the choice of color had been an attempt to stimulate something else, but he also had a notion that bringing up the choice of color was Sara's way of justifying her tears and of hiding the true reason for them. He decided to avoid the sensitive topic, and so the bike stayed untouched in the living room the whole Sunday. When Monday had almost passed as well, Michael couldn't take it anymore.

"Let's go out and try your new bike!" he said. "I'm sure you're going to master it in no time, and if you just give it a few tries we can eat the rest of the Easter candy when we return home." Michael hoped his badly disguised bribe wouldn't put her off. Maybe it did; maybe it didn't. Anyway, in the end Sara reluctantly followed him outside.

Unsurprisingly, they didn't get off to a good start. Sara couldn't flip up the kickstand on her own, so Michael had to help her with that. Then she said she felt awkward leading the bike since the pedals hit her shins, so Michael ended up doing that for her too. Michael felt odd as he led the bike onto a small square close to their apartment building where neighboring kids were playing. A few of them were already riding bikes, and Michael reluctantly noted that some of those kids where a lot younger than his daughter.

"Don't you just love springtime? It's so nice seeing the kids' joy when winter is over and they can finally ride their bikes again!" one mother said, oblivious to how Michael and Sara felt about the situation. Michael managed to mobilize an uncomfortable smile while his daughter kept her eyes fixed firmly on the ground. He felt embarrassed and blamed himself. He couldn't shake the feeling, but he saw no other option, so he soldiered on. "Come on. Let's try this thing!" he said, attempting to psych himself and his daughter up, hoping she couldn't see through his feigned positive attitude. "Let's go! I know you can do this!"

"But I can't even lead the bike! I won't be able to do this on my own. You know that, right? If I get on the bike, do you promise not to let go, Daddy?" Sara asked, looking him in the eyes.

"Don't worry about that part," Michael responded. "This is not that hard. You'll see!"

Sara put her foot over the crossbar and sat on the saddle. Michael walked bent like a penknife, struggling hard for well over an hour to hold Sara upright. He cursed himself for being overconfident and cheap. The guy in the bicycle store had offered to mount a trainer handle on the bike for an extra forty dollars. That would have allowed Michael to push and to hold the bike straight without bending his back, but he had turned down the offer. As time went by, the pain in his back increased, and so did his irritation over the fact that his daughter seemed to put hardly any energy into pedaling or keeping her balance. Everything was up to him. In fact, Sara seemed quite uninvolved as she sat in her saddle. Michael went to great lengths to reinforce even her smallest effort and did his best not to notice the other kids and parents who witnessed their struggle.

"Okay, let's take a break," Michael said when he couldn't bear the pain in his back any longer. When the bike had come to a complete stop, he let go of the carrier and straightened his back. He didn't take time to check whether his daughter had put down her feet (he was too angry over the whole situation to care), and when he removed his support, Sara and the bike fell over.

Sara started crying, and instead of a learning experience that built her confidence, the afternoon turned into yet another blow to her self-esteem. To top things off, in a rare display of frustration, Sara screamed that she would never ride a bike again, especially one that was impossible to keep straight like the one her parents had given her! She ran home and left Michael alone with the bike and the neighbors, who were all trying hard to look as if they weren't watching.

Despite frequent attempts to get her back in the saddle, Sara refused. Weeks passed and the bike remained parked outside their house. Michael was used to being on top of things, but the situation was out of control. As a loving father, he wanted to help his daughter to grow and to learn new things, but he couldn't find a way forward. The only thing that grew now was his feeling of powerlessness. Most of their interactions seemed to leave him and his daughter with a bitter aftertaste, and Michael even felt his good intentions being questioned. Time passed. Summer was around the corner.

"Why do adults lie?" Sara asked. The question yanked Michael out of his daydreaming and into reality. He was sitting at the table with his two daughters, the sun was setting, and they were having a late-evening snack. His wife was at yoga class. Michael had heard Sara's question but couldn't get his head around it.

"What do you mean, darling?" he asked. She stirred the cereal in her bowl. "My preschool teachers lie, and they are the ones telling us we shouldn't." Waiting in vain for her father's guidance, she said, "I don't think it's fair, because when they lie, they just complicate things."

"Well, that doesn't sound right. If that's really the case, we should talk to them about it tomorrow," Michael said wearily and with no intention of forwarding the accusation. He hoped and assumed the issue wouldn't come up again, but it did less than twenty-four hours later. As Michael picked up Sara from preschool after work the following day, by chance he witnessed something that most people wouldn't have seen as dramatic or even special but that would become one of the major epiphanies of his life.

Entering through the door to the preschool, he saw his daughter sitting on the cold stone floor. She didn't notice him as he was at the far end of the corridor, but from where he stood, he could tell she was fretful and defeated. A preschool teacher sat on a bench with a toddler on her lap a few yards away and had her back to his daughter. They were preparing to go outside, and as the teacher dressed the child she tried to talk Sara into putting on her new—and Velcro-free—shoes by herself. "Honey, what do you mean you can't? Of course you can! Come on! Just put some effort into it, and you'll see. You'll make it!"

As Michael watched his daughter from a distance, the realization suddenly overwhelmed him. It was as if someone had punched him in the gut, and he gasped for air. For the first time since the agony over the new bike, he could see how his presence had turned Sara into something less than she was. Michael had gained access to his daughter's perspective, and from there he saw how grown-ups messed things up by insisting on what wasn't true and how his daughter was diminished by being told that her way of seeing reality was wrong.

Michael entered the scene. "Hello, sweetheart," he said, kneeling next to Sara. He gave her a hug and was happy to feel her hug him back. Then he said, "I know you can't tie your shoes on your own, and that's completely okay, you know. Do you want me to show you how to do it so you can learn?" Michael saw Sara's frustration vanish as she nodded affirmatively. Just as he'd done when they'd bought her shoes, Michael demonstrated tying her left shoe and then helped Sara tie the right one herself. As he stood up, he noticed he was not the only one holding his head higher.

Relief. That's what Michael felt walking home with his daughter that day. He couldn't read her mind, but he knew she felt it too. In her face, in her body language, it was obvious that his simple acknowledgment of her inability—the inability to tie her shoes on her own— had transformed his daughter into a different person. Actually, Sara had become herself again. At last, she was again allowed to be her true self—unable to do certain things but eager to learn. The transformation required only that Michael share Sara's view of reality, confirming that it was valid and that he loved her regardless of what that reality looked like.

Michael, eager to demonstrate his abilities as a father— wanting to show the world that he was on top of the situation, that he could control every aspect of his life, including his daughter—had unconsciously denied any fact that might create cracks in his hero facade. The realization that he had unnecessarily put this burden on his back embarrassed Michael, but even more painful was the recognition that in struggling with his own inability to help her learn quickly, he had made his daughter feel that her inability was not okay.

All along, he had assumed that Sara had felt bad about not being able to ride a bicycle, but she hadn't, not until she realized he did. His words and actions had told Sara that her inability would turn her into a victim and that he was desperate for her to be a hero. But Sara had refused his view. She had stood up for herself and for her sound perspective. For her, being a helpless victim at times was just a part of life. From that position she could gradually expand her control and grow up to be the master of her own life—a true hero.

With this new insight, Michael became okay with the situation as it was. He gradually lost desire to control other people's expectations and reactions. His relationship with Sara changed. When Michael felt his daughter had expanded her sphere of control and didn't require his support to stay upright, he now and then let go of the trainer handle[13] with her permission. And that was it. She soon rode the bike on her own. Sara's biking skills were far from perfect. She still wasn't totally in control, but Michael assisted her, and she reached the stage where this was enough for her to progress at her own pace. She fell quite a few times, hurt herself, and got scared, but to the parties involved, that now was okay.

Michael and his wife made sure Sara understood she didn't have to ride the bike to make her parents feel good. They didn't pressure her or tell her lies about the importance of quickly getting back in the saddle again; nobody panicked over feeling out of control for a little while. When the grown-ups supporting her were okay with Sara being afraid, she could seek their comfort when she needed it. With constant access to that safe haven, she could develop her own ways of handling fear.

When Michael changed his perspective, he noticed that Sara shared more openly with him her inabilities and the things that scared her. He also noticed that

---

[13] Yes, he finally bought one.

her verbalizations and acknowledgments made her less afraid and helped her learn. Michael realized he had not been able to accept losing control and thus had lost a great deal of self-esteem as a parent. Now he proudly watched his daughter do her thing at her own pace, and that pace turned out to be faster than Michael could ever have imagined, though this was not important anymore. He gained a sense of fulfillment from handing responsibility to Sara and letting her exercise it at a rate she decided for herself. At this point, all that was required from him was that he do nothing except to be there to comfort her when she needed him.

Almost a year later, on Easter Sunday, crossing the little square between the store and their apartment building, Michael observed a man teaching his son how to ride a bike. He was careful not to stare but couldn't help noticing how the boy's eyes were wet with tears. Michael also noticed how the boy seemed all too aware that this wouldn't be an acceptable time to start crying. Clenching his teeth as was required of him, the boy struggled hard to please his father, who nevertheless looked deeply ashamed and disappointed.

"Come on. Be a big boy! If you don't learn how to do this, your friends will leave you behind when they go on bike trips," Michael heard the man saying.

Hang in there, kid, Michael thought. *Your dad will get it eventually.*

* * *

Everyone loves the hero. He[14] is so popular that most stories make him the center of attention throughout the tale. The hero fixes this, and the hero solves that; no wonder we all want to be him. One of the most firmly established archetypes, the hero with his endless power and ability is always in control as we all wish we could be. If we could control everything all the time there would be nothing we couldn't do. The hero never finds himself out of control, and even when we as spectators, readers, listeners, or moviegoers believe that the hero has—like a regular person—lost control, he always regains it through some courageous or brilliant feat. Those feats usually make up the central part of the story: Ulysses tying himself to the mast so he is not misled by the mesmerizing song of the Sirens; James Bond against all odds escaping a pool that his enemy has filled with sharks. In the hero saga, even when all hope seems lost, the hero always finds a way to change the circumstances in his favor.

The rest of us are all powerless victims of circumstances at times. This doesn't make us bad or incompetent people; it only shows that we're human. For some though, that's not enough. Some people hate being victims so much that when they find themselves in situations where they have no control—stuck in a traffic jam, for example—they do just about anything not to acknowledge what is happening. They do irrational things like screaming at the other drivers caught in the same

---

[14] Yes, in most contemporary stories the hero is still a he, but every now and then it's a Pocahontas.

situation, hitting the horn, and quarreling with the people in the car with them, all because they do not at any cost want to be victims! The truth is that they are the victims of a traffic jam and have no control whatsoever. Hitting the horn and quarreling are just ways of diverting their attention from this obvious fact. Ironically, resisting that they have no control only results in further loss of control.

Another kind of person is quick to embrace circumstances, accepting the fact that although he was completely in control of his life a few moments ago, he has suddenly become a powerless victim. He looks at his watch, curses perhaps, picks up his phone, calls his boss or colleagues, and says, "Look, I'm sorry but I'm caught in a traffic jam, and there is nothing I can do about it. I don't even know when I'll get there." *Voila!* He is now free to recline his seat, turn on the radio, take a sip from his coffee cup, and watch the clouds move across the sky. Contrary to the other guy, screaming and going crazy, this guy stopped being a victim the moment he embraced the fact that the situation was no longer under his control.

You ask a colleague for advice one day, and the next day someone comes to your desk asking for a helping hand. It's no big deal. In a well-functioning relationship or organization, we all take turns being the weak victim and the strong hero. When this process is running smoothly, it is barely noticeable. When it isn't, however, problems will be abundant, and that's just the way desperate heroes like it, because if there were no problems there would be no need for heroes.

This is also why many heroes prefer to monopolize their powers. If everyone had their powers there would be no victims to save. By refusing to share the burden of solving problems and to let go of control, heroes keep others down and remain on top. Indeed, if someone around you is a constant hero, you know you're stuck in a costly dynamic. From the outside, it might look like the hero is helping the victims, and if the roles are only temporary and you're free to alternate, that's probably the case. If the roles are permanent, however, and the victims are forced to stay victims to please a constant hero, the situation will never improve. The problems to solve, the fires to extinguish, the crises to handle, will arise again and again, because if they were removed permanently, the hero wouldn't be required.

So how do you restore a healthy dynamic in which anyone can access special powers when the situation calls for it? How do you make sure recurring problems are eliminated together with the need for someone to constantly act the hero? Well, you help the desperate hero see that in his reluctance ever to be a victim, he has turned himself into the biggest victim of all. Constantly carrying collective burdens, unable to say "I can't make it on my own," automatically sacrificing himself for the greater good, he has become unfree and a constant victim of circumstances that he himself has been part of creating. The only way the constant hero can become free is to allow himself to be saved, to deliberately assume the role of the victim from time to time, and to make room for others to step up to be heroes when required. With access to the full spectrum, from hero to victim and back again, individuals and the organizations they form will improve in the most powerful way.

Every recovering addict is familiar with the victim-hero dynamic. In fact, accepting powerlessness is the first step in the twelve-step program of Alcoholics Anonymous. This step is as crucial as it is hard. Every natural instinct cries out against the idea of personal powerlessness, but accepting that you are powerless is also the first step toward regaining control over your life. This principle applies not only to addicts but to every situation in which a human being has lost control.

Sara knew all this in her gut, and therefore she stood her ground. Without words, she told that incredibly tall dad of hers, his shoulders reaching all the way to the clouds, to embrace the fact that there were things she couldn't do yet or entirely control. That she didn't yet know how to ride a bike was not embarrassing. Even if this fact turned her into a victim, and even if that fact made her dad feel like a victim, it was the truth, and she was okay with that. Sara loved her dad regardless and expected the same from him. She knew she could regain her control over the situation only by accepting that there were things she couldn't control, and this is the truth we call the paradox of suckcess.

CHAPTER 5

*The Moldy Scientist
Who Thrived in the Dark*

BECOMING A GENIUS BY EMBRACING YOUR INNER FOOL

We think of Marie Curie as a genius, but she wasn't always revered. During her lifetime, French newspapers would publish accounts of what a fool she was, building a hatred so strong against her that she ended up having to flee the country. It wasn't until Curie stopped fearing the foolishness within that she and her discoveries could demand the respect they deserved and go on to change human history.

THE ONLY THING MR. SKLODOWSKI HATED
more than the Russian tsar was foolishness. He hated
foolishness so much that he would dedicate all his waking
hours to endlessly tutoring his children, driving out any
silliness as soon as possible and replacing it with aware-
ness, poise, and knowledge. Mr. Sklodowski had been on
the cusp of building a career in science in his homeland of
Poland, but his high hopes had been crushed by politics,
and as every Polish attempt to overthrow the Russian
oppressors failed, he perceived himself to be locked up
economically, intellectually, and emotionally. He believed
his hands, no matter how nimble, were tied.

No wonder, then, that pride and an acute sense of its loss
dominated the Sklodowski residence. To their loving father,
anything ingenious produced by his children was proof that
he was right and society wrong. Any sign of foolishness, on
the other hand, meant a battle lost, and so, although Mr.
Sklodowski proudly displayed his science research tools to
the bewilderment and admiration of his children, he left no
room for experimenting, playing or goofing around. Within
the four walls of the Sklodowski home, ingenuity was all that
mattered. "In our family, we were born gifted … We should

all be thankful. Never ever let me catch you acting like fools," the father told his children.

Mr. Sklododowski's wife passed away early, and Marie, the youngest of the five children, was eager to win the approval of her surviving parent. The obvious way would be to prove herself as a science genius, but this was the eighteen hundreds and the opportunities for young girls looking for careers in science were scarce, to say the least. Besides, Marie's father was unable to support an academic education for any of his children. Marie and her sister, who against all odds was aiming to be a doctor, made a pact to follow their dreams anyway, and in 1891 Marie took off for Paris, leaving her beloved but demanding father behind, at least in geographical terms.

One might expect that moving from a small town in Poland to Paris, considered the center of the Western world, would be an exhilarating experience for a young person, but for Marie the move was not a goal but a means to an end. Her aim was to leave a lasting mark on science, but if circumstances had been dismal in Poland they were no better in France. To support even a lifestyle stripped of superfluous comfort, she needed to work long hours in the homes of Parisian families, spending her nights studying. She would drag heavy sacks of coal along the streets, past the partying crowds and up the stairs, fueling her little bedside stove to keep warm on winter nights. She would gather her clothes to use as a bedcover.

Marie had no ambition to become a perfect wife and couldn't have cared less about how to make a pie; in fact, she didn't care much about food at all. She shunned typical life—the parties, the recklessness, the fun, the dancing, the heartaches, the interaction with other people—for ingenuity. Marie was one of only two women at the University of Sorbonne, and with the words of her father ringing in her head, she did everything in her power to make sure she was always the top student. She was so competitive and uncomfortable around the other students that she said social events like dance parties held absolutely no interest for her. In fact, she said, all the dancing was making people around her look as stupid as the parties they attended.

One might expect such an elitist personality never to marry, but fate led Marie to meet a young man with a scholarly ambition matching her own. She and Pierre Curie became partners in science as much as anything, constantly collaborating and supporting each other as equals. However, as Pierre was a man and Marie a woman at a time when women were expected only to care for the household and the children, Pierre was offered esteemed positions and a nice laboratory whereas Marie ended up pursuing her dreams in an improvised underground laboratory that looked like a potato cellar—a dark, smelly and moldy place. In fact, it was such a gruesome space that upon visiting, Marie and Pierre's daughter labeled it "the sad place." Their daughter wasn't the only one shocked at the poor conditions in Marie's workplace.

The only person unfazed about having to spend time there was Marie Curie. It may not have looked like much to others, but this was her private space, and in great contrast with the laboratories staffed by proud and ambitious men, in that potato cellar, society's constraints did not apply. Below ground, supervised by no one, Marie was free to investigate the most distant scientific possibilities, even the seemingly foolish ones. Pierre helped her obtain strange minerals from faraway countries, and with this material in her possession, Marie would look for things nobody else would be crazy enough to believe existed. Still, reports from visitors were troubling. Like some gloomy old witch, Marie stirred giant pots of strangely glowing pitchblende,[15] and she would do so for hours on end until she was exhausted. To the uninvolved, it all seemed like the doings in a mad house. Wasn't this so-called laboratory the refuge of a crazy person, the dark and stinking space of a fool?

But with constant access to her own space, Marie Curie was happy, and in that cellar she would bloom. While her male contemporaries had to worry about building their résumés, Marie Curie and her explorations were of no concern to anybody. Unbothered by which way of doing things was considered proper for a genius, she was free to follow her silly whims and to engage in as many irrational escapades as she wanted, making discoveries no one else could. And yet her father's words echoed in her mind, demanding that she never be anything but a

---

[15] Pitchblende, or *pechblände*, was a raw mix of minerals brought up out of the ground in certain areas, including parts of Austria. Because of its radioactivity, pitchblende was the raw material Marie Curie needed to do her experiments, and Pierre would pull strings to help her get it.

genius, turning her into something smaller and more constrained than she really was. In addition, because women and science were a strange and threatening combination, men of science were constantly questioning her, and she hated it.

Eventually, all those men had to do was call her a fool and she would comply. The more she struggled not to seem silly or strange, the more easily she was manipulated. As an example, it took her many years of heavy, dangerous work to extract even a tiny gram of radium from tons of pitchblende, and still, when another scientist showed up on her doorstep and demanded that she produce that same amount of radium for him to use (for free!), she immediately made herself busy doing just that. One might expect that winning the Nobel Prize would have served as some kind of acknowledgment for Marie Curie, a triumphant moment, a big step up the ladder, but it didn't. Furthermore, when out of "diplomatic concerns" the Nobel committee decided that the prize should be shared by Henri Becquerel and Pierre Curie,[16] Marie did not even object. Only after Pierre protested was Marie added as a recipient.

---

[16] Not that Pierre himself cared much for glory. On the contrary, he would not miss an opportunity to point out that his wife was the true genius. When informed about the unfair views of the Swedish prize committee, he immediately wrote a letter to the committee demanding that Marie at least be one of the persons awarded. Committee members accepted but in the end decided to give 50 percent of the prize money to Becquerel and the other half to Pierre, saying Marie—to them, primarily Pierre's wife—would this way get some money as well.

Instead of demanding the glory that was hers, she got busy again, hurrying back to her cellar to put in more hours and mixing that hard work with the right amount of fooling around. After another eight years the discoveries she'd made were so great that the Nobel committee had no choice but to give her a second award. This time, however, the men in the sunlight joined forces to shove her back into the ground.

The one person who backed her up was Pierre. Proud of her achievements, he used to carry in his pocket bits of radium to hold up in the dusk at parties to impress the other guests with its mystical, radioactive glow. He also was the first to suffer from its lethal powers. Already in a poor state because of diseases related to the exposure, Pierre crossed the street in disarray and was run over by traffic. He died soon after. Marie was crushed. She gradually recovered over the years, and by the time she got the news about winning the Nobel Prize one more time she had been romantically involved with the married scientist Paul Langevin[17] for quite some time.

When Langevin's wife found out about the affair she was terribly upset. She contacted the press and quotes from the letters were published in the French papers. Contrary to what contemporary mores might have us

---

[17] Langevin famously came to a similar conclusion on relativity as Einstein did, only he did so later. At the time, letters were the common way of correspondence, and living in a different area, Langevin had not yet learned about what Einstein had presented. When he realized Einstein had covered the same ground only weeks before him, he was devastated.

assume, people were not primarily blaming Monsieur Langevin, the married party in the affair, but the widowed Marie Curie, who was vehemently attacked from every direction possible. The foulest verbal assaults came from her male scientist competitors, who called her crazy and a fool. The American radiochemistry scientist Bertram Boltwood was quoted as saying, "She is exactly what I always thought she was; a detestable idiot."[18]

Fueled by extensive reports in the papers, prejudice against Marie Curie built quickly. People threw rocks at the windows of her home, and soon Marie, like some old village idiot, was expelled from Paris. One would assume that having discovered radioactivity, polonium, and radium—each find far greater than any contemporary scientist could dream of—she would have been a celebrated member of society. She named the element polonium to honor her father and her native country of Poland; the name of Poland would forever appear in the periodic table studied by science scholars, but not even old Mr. Sklodowski was impressed. Instead, he claimed that his daughter's discovery of radium "would never amount to any real significance outside the limited field of science."

The Nobel committee, having announced Marie's second win before the scandal of the Langevin romance erupted, now out of fear urged her not to show up for the

---

[18] For a more extensive account, see the *Obsessive Genius: The Inner World of Marie Curie* by Barbara Goldsmith.

prize ceremony, and so, bit by bit, the foolishness that Marie Curie had learned to fear had come to define her in the eyes of others. She had done everything she could to prove her detractors wrong, but as time passed she had become less able to convince even herself. For her, science had proven to be about exploring crazy possibilities to make ingenious findings; without making room for foolishness there would be no space for ingenuity. Indeed, it appears that around this time, Marie Curie had slowly started to accept being considered a fool, because although she was in a bad state and the journey from Paris to Stockholm was long and exhausting, she made the foolish move of attending the Nobel Prize ceremony, ignoring the committee's plea to stay away.

Winning the prize the previous time, she had been too concerned about avoiding ridicule even to take credit for her work. A woman in the male domain of science, she would never fit the mold of the scientific genius. She was far out of place, and to hide that fact she kept a low profile, expressed her gratitude with a curtsy, and made sure not to embarrass herself even more by revealing her unconventional approaches or by blowing her own horn and inviting criticism.

As she received her second Nobel Prize, however, Marie Curie did the exact opposite. Having spent a lifetime resisting being a fool in the eyes of others—her father, fellow students, other scientists, journalists—she finally succumbed. Instead of denying its existence, she let her inner fool out of the cellar and into the world. She gave herself permission to act like the detestable idiot people had so forcefully claimed her to be. Delivering that unwanted speech in Stockholm, she could finally play the entire fool-genius spectrum as she pleased. The fool and the genius—yes, that's what she was! Clad in a woolen dress in a world where everyone else was wearing a tail coat, having made discoveries strange enough to keep humanity occupied for decades, she impolitely took full credit for her accomplishments, unconventionally pointing out their huge implications, claiming her own genius the way only a fool would. And that's when she broke through.

People went completely nuts. Change came with the force of a tidal wave that flushed away Marie Curie's deteriorating reputation and elevated her to the skies. As she embraced and celebrated her own genius, others did too. From then on, people hoping to communicate that they were serious about science wanted to add her name to whatever they were doing. Soon enough, streets, schools, and institutes would honor her achievements, and Marie Curie is now a statue on a pedestal.[19] If you ask about the gloomy old fool in the potato cellar, however, chances are no one will know whom you are talking about.

One would like to think Marie Curie once and for all defeated the oppressive structure, the one that because of our desire for ingenuity keeps us all afraid of foolishness, but unfortunately, things soon returned to normal.

---

[19] There are plenty of statues of Marie Curie, one in Paris and one in Warsaw shimmering like gold, to name a few.

Marie Curie may have torn down quite a bit of the gender barrier that used to keep women out of the realms of science, but when it comes to the foolishness at the heart of the matter, no one seems aware of her achievements, and so the old order still limits our scope.

The paradox of suckcess is that to achieve success, you must not let fear of what is on the other end of the scale limit you. In the case of Marie Curie and her quest for ingenuity, however, foolishness was perceived as a major threat, and crossing the imagined boundary between the two, she was perceived as dangerous not just to her competitors but to the order of society. We all like to think that with time, things change for the better, and maybe it is so, but the illusory conflict between being a fool and a genius persists and is as misleading as ever. Just as in the days of Marie Curie's breakthroughs, it is today widely believed that the best way to achieve the ingenious is by laboring to make sure foolishness does not rear its ugly head. The history books of our time reflect our values. To stand as an example for the kind of future we believe is best for our children, we need an unalloyed female genius, and so Marie Curie goes down in history as nothing but a genius.

Considering the implications of Marie Curie's discovery of radium, her father's deprecating words sound like a joke. Apart from that other discovery of hers—radioactivity, which paved the way for nuclear power—it is hard to imagine a discovery that has had greater impact on humanity than the discovery of radium. This element has saved human lives time and time again, both as the essential ingredient in the X-ray process and as the only effective means of treating patients suffering from otherwise deadly cancer. Before X-rays and radium were used correctly in combination, surgeons had to dig bullets out of wounded soldiers by guessing. Through the foolish genius of Marie Curie, however, they could take photos and see the damaged insides of war victims—the bullets, the shrapnel, the broken bones—saving an unmeasurable number of lives.

*   *   *

Fear, it seems, is central here. People like to give the impression that they love to think outside the box, that they love challenges, that they are keen to explore new ways of doing things, but are they? Or, in saying those things, are they trying to build respectable careers by fitting the mold? We don't mean to say that people deliberately lie about their ambitions, but we suspect that when convention and invention do not match, most will pick the former. One could argue that we have come a long way since the eighteen hundreds, but social pressure to conform remains strong. To give you a telling example, we don't have to leave Stockholm.

Simon Kyaga[20] has an aura of trustworthiness. He is a chief physician in psychiatry, has a neat appearance,

---

[20] Apart from being chief physician in psychiatry at Karolinska Institutet in Stockholm, Simon Kyaga is also the author of *Creativity and Mental Illness*. Kyaga shares some of his findings on the relationship between genius and madness in this TEDx-talk: https://youtu.be/EIWxnISAiQY?list=PL1047FC9FEDD4900B.

and talks in a thoughtful manner, giving the impression that every syllable is fact-checked before leaving his lips. Science (not necessarily the area in which he currently conducts research) seems to be his passion in life. His boyish smile and the constant glint in his eyes almost feel a bit out of character, but putting one and one together you realize that they are merely manifestations of the curiosity that has fueled one of the sharpest medical minds of our time.

When we met Kyaga for lunch at a century-old brasserie in central Stockholm, he told us how one of the oldest myths of Western society—the idea of a link between the genius and the crazy fool—became his major field of research when he was presented with a unique opportunity to once and for all determine whether this link was a scientific fact or not.

Sweden has been known as a gold mine for the study of diseases. We have Swedish bureaucracy to thank for that. Sweden was one of the first countries to introduce a system of individually unique personal registration numbers and has a two-century tradition of collecting and storing individual epidemiologic data. This data can be found in other places, but nowhere else in the world is the quality of the data so high and uniform, and above all, nowhere else is the amount of data gathered on mental illness large enough to support significant scientific research on the topic.

So Kyaga got down to business. Like any scientist, he started by assuming the myth would prove to be bust.

When performing scientific experiments, your default position should always be that there is no relationship between two measured phenomena. Hence Kyaga started with the hypothesis that there was no link between being a genius and a fool before diving into the data to see whether there were grounds to reject the hypothesis. This approach is analogous to a criminal trial in which the defendant is assumed to be innocent until proven guilty beyond reasonable doubt. In the world of statistics, reasonable doubt is normally translated into limiting the risk of erroneously discarding a hypothesis to 5 percent, but as it turned out, the myth was proven a scientific fact.

After analyzing data from almost three hundred thousand patients and their relatives, Kyaga eliminated all doubt. The genius and the fool really do walk hand in hand, and to most of us the result doesn't seem all that surprising. What's harder to grasp is how Kyaga's results were received by fellow scientists.

The resistance was fierce. All articles sent to scientific journals for publication are reviewed by other researchers, and it's not unusual to be questioned and asked to fill in any blanks. For Kyaga, though, the process became nothing less than Kafkaesque. The article describing his research and results was rejected repeatedly without reasonable explanation. He turned to journal after journal, often receiving only one word in response: rejected. When one journal responded with thirty-five objections, he saw this as progress. Having gone to great lengths to respond to each of those objections with clarifications and further analysis, Kyaga sent a revised version of his scientific paper. The response was concise: rejected.

Many of the researchers who scrutinized Kyaga's article gave the impression of being against his findings per se, and it would take more than a year of further analysis and rewriting before the seven-page article was finally accepted for publication.[21] This did not end the protests, though. Instead it became obvious that stating that a human being can hold two seemingly contrary traits at the same time still was a threat to the old scientific dogma. Fortunately, with the proof presented by Kyaga, the insight that one side of the spectrum (ingenuity) can coexist with the other (foolishness) finally got recognition.

Still, as Kyaga remarked as we parted after lunch, one shouldn't be surprised if people continue to defend the view that it can be only one or the other, because that is what we are used to thinking. What we call common sense often limits our ability to make correct scientific conclusions. We are comfortable thinking that a fool and a genius can never be the same person, and we do not like it when someone suggests we adopt a different view. In Kyaga's experience it's perfectly normal for people to react defensively toward threats against their worldview, and the larger the threat, the stronger the opposition. Even so, the people who opposed Kyaga's

---

[21] "Creativity and mental disorder: family study of 300,000 people with severe mental disorder," the first article based on Kyaga's research on the link between madness and creativity, was published in *The British Journal of Psychiatry* in 2011.

findings were scholars, and as such they should have been prepared to accept any fact presented as long as it was scientifically solid. Instead, Kyaga and his colleagues ran into stubborn opposition. Why?

Well, here is a plausible reason. Defining the madness part of the study had been quite easy—Kyaga had used the diagnoses of mental illness found in the epidemiologic data. The genius part had been more of a challenge, but in the end, Kyaga and his team decided to define genius as "having some kind of job that demands higher levels of creativity and possibly intelligence," and among the jobs defined as such was that of the researcher himself. Kyaga's inquiry revealed a link running straight from high-status, scientific-scholar geniuses to the very low-status fools examined—and the other way back again. For other researchers, that was too much to swallow. The scientific approach used by Kyaga and his colleagues was impeccable, but that didn't matter. What did matter was that Kyaga's research threatened the identity of an entire profession, and so it comes as no surprise that the article met such strong opposition. Sadly, what the researchers who reject the findings do not realize is that, by denying their inner fools, they constrain the powers of their genius.

The fool and the genius possess the same traits—unconventional thinking, stubbornness, going places where no one else goes, impatience, occasional tunnel vision, and a penchant for asking inconvenient questions. When things are done right and with courage, those traits are often found in one and the same person—and probably within you if the people around you permit it and if you have the guts to let it happen. If you find yourself in an emotional struggle between feeling like a genius one moment and a fool the next, let go and realize that there was no conflict to begin with. As the fool and the genius overlap to such a great extent, one cannot exist without the other. Consequently, accessing the powers of your inner genius is all about letting the inner fool out of its moldy cellar asylum.

CHAPTER 6

The Sleepless Rocket Engineer Who Fell from the Sky

BECOMING A BELIEVER
BY EMBRACING YOUR
INNER SCEPTIC

During the Cold War, exploring space was part of a quest for supremacy on the ground, and as such, shooting rockets into the sky with people in them was part of greater patriotic ambition. Right from the start, space endeavors were seen as unreal, and it was widely understood that to do the impossible, you had to believe. Allan J. McDonald, the protagonist of this story, would prove to be a die-hard believer, but because he was also a skeptic, he worried about things to which others turned a blind eye. In 1986, as matters went from bad to worse, the reason for McDonald's worries was broadcast in dead silence on national television.

ALLAN J. MCDONALD ISN'T A BIG NAME. With his gray hair, office shoes, clean-shaven face, and unremarkable accent, he doesn't stand out in a crowd. You hear his name, and five minutes later you hear it again and ask your friend who this Allan person is. Fortunately, McDonald's claim to fame isn't in his appearance but in the work he did and in the major event of which he was a part.

Much later McDonald would write a book about the whole thing: what exactly happened, what preceded it, what the aftermath was, who blamed whom, who said what. The book is more than six hundred pages long, and with no offense to McDonald, it isn't the kind of book you bring to the beach on a holiday.[22] Quite the opposite, McDonald's story relies on thorough explanations of things like field joint designs. It includes long, unexplained abbreviations and lists of names mentioned for reasons that remain obvious only to him, and when he recalls an episode thirty years ago, kind of like how one's

---

[22] *Truth, Lies and O-Rings* was published in 2003 and offers probably the most thorough rundown on the matter, though not the only one.

grandfather would, no detail is too small or irrelevant. So you read the book a page at a time, and if after a few months you still haven't given up, chances are you will when you see the black-and-white pictures of things like the SRM-16A nozzle joint primary O-rings.

In short, it's rocket science, and most likely you've never heard of Allan J. McDonald before. Don't be embarrassed. He is never included in any school or history books, and as a digital example of his obscurity, *Wikipedia* lists as many as eighteen notable men named Allan McDonald, and none of them is this guy.

A lot of times you hear people say something like "Yeah, it can be easily done. It isn't exactly rocket science!" And when a passenger on a platform has been waiting too long for the train to arrive, he or she will say, "They can put a man on the moon, but they still can't get the bloody trains to run on time!" To work with rockets and spacecraft, you need to master advanced knowledge, to be meticulous, and to be fully committed to what you are doing. In short, space just isn't for clowns.

Also, you need to be more than just one person. When a space rocket is built, thousands of people are involved, all of them experts in their fields, and the rocket is the result of one grand, proud collaboration. Collaboration isn't possible without communication. However, few people have both excellent engineering skills and superior communication skills, and it is safe to assume that NASA doesn't hire engineers mainly for their exceptional ability to communicate but for what they know about things like nozzle joints. Engineering comes first and then, somewhere on the candidate's list of skills, the agency hopes to find the ability to communicate in a professional manner.

To most of us it would seem that communicating and being able to speak one's heart are as crucial as anything when working together, and space rockets should be no exception. We can all agree that if communication is somehow clogged or compromised the result will be flawed as well. What if something goes wrong and isn't fixed? What if only a few people know about the problem and for some reason—fear of punishment, for example—keep quiet about it? The flaws generated by such a failure to communicate will be bad for any endeavor, but for space rockets, they can be fatal.

For those who weren't around on January 28, 1986, there is always *YouTube*, although watching this episode is horrifying. Also, chances are you already know the outcome, and so you realize the countdown is no less than a national trauma waiting to happen.

The people in the movie clip, however, initially see this as a day of national pride and celebration. When the space rocket finally takes off, onlookers are cheering. "Here we go! This is it! That is my daughter/mother/wife/sister/son/father/husband/brother inside that rocket, going into space!" And apparently there's no problem to begin with. Knowing what's next, it is quite hard not to be surprised at how smoothly everything seems to be running until seventy-three seconds after the launch, and even then, depending on which clip you pick, the reactions of reporters and NASA people are rather subdued.

Viewers can see a big, shocking explosion in the sky. Debris is flying everywhere and there are great lines of smoke. And this probably is the worst part: even after the catastrophe has happened, most bystanders are still smiling, looking at the sky in excited bewilderment. There is not a shadow of a doubt—there never was! They have all grown used to believing, and they are sure the rocket with their loved ones inside is still on its way into space. They were not skeptics before, and even though the rocket explodes before them they have no intention of allowing skepticism to ruin things now. After another moment has passed, however, the discrepancy between what ought to be and what is actually happening becomes unbearable. The spectators now look to each other for guidance but find no one there to guide them.

After a long wait, a space center announcer finally says something about "a major malfunction," and still, instead of responding by screaming, crying, or gasping for air, people wait curiously to see what will happen next.[23] It is not until the painfully flat voice finally says "it has been confirmed that the vehicle has exploded" that people start to look troubled. They all saw it happen, but what difference does that make when everyone long ago agreed to believe no matter what? When the worst possible scenario takes place before their eyes, they all wait

---

[23] https://www.youtube.com/watch?v=WDRxK6cevqw

for some kind of authority to tell them whether what they just saw was real. Their gut feeling is gone. It's not just the crowd at the space center. If, for example, you watch CNN's live broadcast,[24] you can hear the reporter, who is supposed to expect the unexpected, going quiet for what seems like an eternity, and then, although the space shuttle has just exploded, he says there is no word on survivors.

The *Challenger* disaster remains one of the great American tragedies. All seven crew members died, and the flaws impossible to speak of before were now brutally exposed for the world to see. The technical explanation was that the O-rings weren't made for the unusually cold temperatures that January morning. Some had worried about icicles on the rocket ramp, but the O-rings had been the bigger concern for Allan McDonald. He was the engineer responsible, and he had been so upset about this possible flaw that he refused to sign the paper equaling a go signal to launch. He had strongly warned that before launching at such cold temperatures, further testing was absolutely necessary. With such great responsibility one cannot and should not rely on good faith. That was his stance.

By refusing to sign, McDonald put his career at stake. This was the last and most formal way of communicating with the rest of the team, his way of saying something might be unacceptably wrong with the rocket, and still the rocket was launched. This could be labeled

---

[24] https://www.youtube.com/watch?v=1rDg7S46ijM

an engineering failure, but the problem was known all along. The engineering team was not in oblivion, but the collective mood was that of the believer, and what McDonald had to say sounded an awful lot like the words of a person at the opposite end of the spectrum—the skeptic.

Still, as the failing parts that had caused the catastrophe were his responsibility, McDonald had to answer a lot of questions. A presidential commission held hearings, and he was the center of attention. He didn't hesitate to spill the beans. This was his opportunity to speak. Finally, things could be set right, and his main point was that up until then, in some respects, NASA and its contractors sucked. He wasn't the only one who knew about the O-ring problem, but even after what had happened, people hated him for not keeping his mouth shut. There were threats, fistfights, and lawsuits. Still, at the center of the storm, McDonald felt he had to tell the truth. He reported that whenever he closed his eyes, he could see the rocket exploding and couldn't look away. People around him wanted to see him fired, and speaking of fire, the wife of one of his former bosses told him she wished she could have the pleasure of seeing McDonald strapped to one of the blazing rocket boosters.

In the end, though, McDonald rode it all out. Having been dragged through the dirt in the litigation process, he came out clean and won his job back. However, because of the skepticism he had shown before the O-ring flaws became evident, his new, nerve-racking job was to redesign the rocket and to put it back on the launching pad.

And so the meticulous McDonald got to work redesigning the defective components. It was no small task. The focal point of national attention, he would be an absent father for many years, and this wasn't the most enjoyable time of his life. In his book, he describes the creepy feeling he had returning to work, not knowing whom to trust. Which people were still his friends, and which people were eager to stab him in the back for having the guts to stand his ground?

Upon returning, however, McDonald learned that many of the people around him, especially those who had accused him of not believing in the project and who had been so keen to criticize him for being a skeptic, had lost faith and were leaving. As time went by, it became evident that McDonald, the skeptic, was also the most devoted believer.

Now this isn't the kind of tale that ends with the protagonist scaling the ranks to be hailed as the king. Dangerous situations occurred again, in part, it seems, because NASA always had to accept the contractor offering the lowest bid. Rank, money, and power remained in the front seat, and in 2003, another rocket exploded. Not on McDonald's watch, though.

Free to pose the important but inconvenient questions when in doubt, McDonald also knew when to fully trust his instincts. Operating both as a skeptic and as a believer, depending on what the situation required of him, McDonald had constant and unlimited access to the full spectrum. Contrary to what his old adversaries had expected, the skeptical McDonald remained adamant in his belief.

His readiness to serve in the space program proved both profound and lasting, and the astronauts on board loved him for it. They said that when they buckled up, the part that worried them the least was the one supervised by McDonald, and history shows they were right. As a skeptic, a believer, or anything in between, he would say whatever needed to be said, and for the next 110 launches, the rocket boosters designed by McDonald came back flawless. And although the image of the *Challenger* exploding in the sky would never quite leave his mind's eye, Allan McDonald finally managed to get a good night's sleep every once in a while.

* * *

Any way you look at it, McDonald did his part. He was the guy who spoils the party, the guy at the meeting who doesn't mind asking one more lengthy question just when all the other attendants are cheerfully getting up to leave.

The dictionary says a skeptic is someone who "habitually questions the authenticity of any accepted belief." That is an apt description of Allan McDonald, and plenty of people still dislike him for it. This is his way of putting it: "In my career, I don't know how many times people have raised their hand and said, 'This may be a dumb question, but ...' I always stood up and said, 'In my entire career I've never, ever heard a dumb question.'"[25]

That is quite an annoying opinion, isn't it? No dumb questions ever? He's got to be joking! There are plenty of fantastic people in this world, but it is also full to the brim with morons, and to hear them all out would be quite tedious. Imagine all the whining and the petty complaints! Picture some old guy in a corner waiting impatiently for his retirement in a few years. Whatever action someone suggests, he won't like it because he just wants to sit around and do nothing.

If this is how you picture the skeptic, however, think again. That whiny old guy should take time off and try to find out what makes him happy, and we hope he does. This is a chapter about the surprising connection between the skeptic and the believer, so sad old man, buy a fishing boat and get out of our text already. Quite contrary to the disheartened clock watcher, the skeptic usually cannot get enough. When everyone else is ready to start believing after a couple of obvious answers have been offered, the skeptic goes on, eager to learn more and to push things further.

Most people can recall knowing something is wrong and being afraid to speak up about it. The problem usually is fear of punishment. You know in your gut

---

[25] http://www.nasa.gov/centers/langley/news/researchernews/rn_Colloquium1012.html

that even if you do the right thing, people will hate you for it. If this was a different kind of book, this would be the part where we tell you to change your mind-set and to choose a more positive outlook, but we won't. That kind of advice is handed out far too often and far too carelessly, with far too serious consequences. We know better than to repeat generic and empty advice that you've already heard, and we know that millions of people are punished every day for refusing to act like believers when the people around them demand it.

Though it might appear a bit contradictory, out of all the world's institutions, it is the Roman Catholic Church that offers a better way forward. In its quest for the truth, the church found it necessary to make sure that when an important decision was made, a skeptical approach would be taken. In the sixteenth century, Vatican officials decided that before they could believe that someone was a saint, they needed to expose that person to the harshest kind of skepticism available. That is how the canonization process came to include a person who argued strongly against the candidate. That person's job was to take the most skeptical view of the candidate possible, to search for any holes in the evidence, and to vehemently argue that any miracles attributed to the person considered for sainthood were fraudulent.

The professional skeptic was popularly titled the devil's advocate, and the expression recalls this old religious function. It is worth noting, however, that devil's advocate was never the term used by the church. Latin was the language of the clergy, and the church called the person in this role *promotor fidei,* which means "promotor of faith." In other words, the true promotor of belief was not someone convinced about the good qualities of the person proposed for sainthood, but the skeptic, whose job it was to run nothing less than a smear campaign against the venerated individual.

This kind of skepticism, protected by rules and traditions, resembles the approach so common in the early Middle Ages when professional clowns called jesters were employed to entertain the court. These court jesters held a unique privilege of freely speaking their minds. This gave jesters the opportunity—and the responsibility—to point out the elephant in the room in a humorous and indirect way. Today this privilege has often been revoked, and all that remains is a king or a queen in oblivion, surrounded by a bunch of clowns who do nothing but applaud. As these clowns are pretty much everywhere these days, so are fatal half-truths, prejudice, and neglect.

The revered nineteenth-century philosopher John Stuart Mill, famous for his defense of individual freedom, believed that freedom of speech was absolutely necessary for any widely held opinion to be considered reliable. Not until an opinion has been exposed to its most frantic opposition can we safely assume that it is wise to let ourselves be guided by that opinion. And even after that, it is safe to do so only while full freedom of speech remains. The moment opposition is limited, our collective truths become hollow and unreliable.[26]

It's understandable that you might hesitate to assume the role of the skeptic, considering how the brave Allan McDonald and people like him have been treated. Proactive leaders know this, and so they appoint people to act as devil's advocates for each meeting or project. Those who see them in action learn that having the guts to be a skeptic transforms a person into someone others trust, rely on, and come to for serious advice. Also, children can more easily relate to a parent who is a skeptic, because such a parent gives them assurance that the negative views and emotions they sometimes hold are okay. If we reject the skeptical views of others, we also reject a part of them, increasing the emotional distance between them and us.

Positive thinking can be a good way to get out of bed in the morning or to muster the courage to ask someone out on a date, but it must not be used as a shield against fruitful skepticism. If positive thinking dictates your every word, you will become unreliable, easy to manipulate, and less interesting to be with. Making plans for a bright future can give you the motivation to continue forward, but when suppressed negativity about the present forces you to constantly overestimate your future

---

[26] "Complete liberty of contradicting and disproving our opinion, is the very condition which justifies us in assuming its truth for purposes of action; and on no other terms can a being with human faculties have any rational assurance of being right." – John Stuart Mill, *On Freedom*, 1859.

prospects, you're in big trouble. Indeed, in 2013, research at the University of Erlangen-Nuremberg in Germany revealed that being overly optimistic when predicting the future was associated with a much greater risk of disability and death within the following decade.[27] The study explained that skepticism encourages people to plan better, take necessary precautions, and make more informed decisions. Simply put, a person who has access to skepticism, belief, and everything in between, will maximize his or her chances of a long, healthy life.

Embracing the paradox of suckcess, we no longer fear skepticism and the possibility that we will be perceived as negative. Then we can finally start addressing real problems instead of mumbling petty complaints about the weather. Furthermore, when our negativity is aimed in the direction where it belongs, we can be positive about the good things in life. Bit by bit, we can reclaim that gut feeling that we have learned to suppress. Earlier, to avoid looking like skeptics, we would remind ourselves to smile no matter how we felt. Now we will smile spontaneously when doing so reflects our true feelings—and yell at people who insist we should launch rockets that haven't been sufficiently tested.

---

[27] The researchers (Lang, Weiss, Gerstorf, and Wagner) examined data on approximately forty thousand people collected annually from 1993 to 2003, and their findings were presented in an article titled "Forecasting Life Satisfaction Across Adulthood: Benefits of Seeing a Dark Future?" published in *Psychology and Aging* in 2013.

CHAPTER 7

*The Lonely Teen
Who Expanded
His Vocabulary*

BECOMING A PIONEER
BY EMBRACING YOUR
INNER REJECT

In this chapter the fourteen-year-old version of David Hirasawa is abroad on a summer language course in the south of England. While jumping around between tables in the lunchroom, he discovers that a quiz that was supposed to be about soccer clubs and Big Ben turns out to be all about the strange connection between being a pioneer and being a reject left behind for all the world to see.

EVERYONE WAS JUMPING TABLES. THE swapping around was fun and a little scary. The tables were placed so that it was possible to skip from one to the next without touching the floor, but we were like a bunch of careless squirrels, tripping and falling and giggling. One girl from the Netherlands hurt her knee, and a guy from Moldova sprained his ankle. (I think he was the only one who could have found Moldova on a world map. We were all fourteen to sixteen, and Moldova, for reasons that make total sense when you are a teenager, seemed a very uncool place to be from.)

The hall we were in was the big space where we gathered for any activity after class, and we ate lunch at the three very large tables. The menu was dominated by English items like Cornwall pie, vinegar-flavored chips, and neon purple grape Jell-O that we would stuff in our backpacks to throw at the passing double decker buses two blocks down the street from the school. There were eighty to a hundred of us, and only about half of what was going on around me made any sense, which meant that most days the world seemed unnervingly irrational and hard to grasp. I was fourteen and skinny. I got drunk for the first time, and to my bafflement, my genitals were growing fast. I knew they would grow, of course; this was puberty, but still.

We were in the hall for the Wednesday afternoon quiz, and the three tables represented the three possible answers to each question. Only one of the three was right, of course. Our teachers—Greg, Sybil, and a person who, for some unknown reason, we called "the Other Guy"— would read questions out loud, and then we all had to decide the answers individually. We weren't allowed to confer, and so we had to be quiet. The questions involved all things British, like the name of the singer in the Rolling Stones, how to correctly address the queen, the capital of Scotland, and so on.

After everyone had chosen a table, Greg would mess things up by saying, "If you want to swap around, swap around now!" We could now change our minds, and we did. There was a lot of table swapping before Greg with great finality read out the correct answer. He would point at the table that was correct, and the kids at the other tables had to step down and watch and wait for the next run. The winner was awarded some ridiculous prize. I can't remember what it was. It didn't matter.

I can't say it crossed my mind that I would get a girlfriend that summer. An Italian guy was staying with the same family I was, and we would sometimes walk a French girl to the door at night after-school discos and such. She was awesome. We were in an old town on the south coast of England, and I would sometimes sit on the beach with a Swedish girl named Eva, but I think trying to kiss her would have ruined the bond of trust between us.

In school there were two Spanish girls, fifteen and sixteen years old, and they stood out from the crowd. They were sun-kissed and seemed comfortable about wearing high-heel espadrilles and sunglasses. They looked like film stars. On one occasion, I asked one of them a question and was surprised and grateful that she didn't frown when I opened my mouth. That was the only time I spoke to either of them, and if someone had shown her a picture of me five minutes later, I don't think she would have remembered who I was. I'm sure there was nothing wrong with her memory, and she wasn't rude or arrogant; on the contrary she was friendly, but that's how small an impression I felt I left. I speculated about what it would take to be with someone like her, and I was convinced that, besides being a few years older than she was, one would have to have a car, be loud-mouthed, strange, and unreliable, and wear pants and shoes with holes in them.

To get us started, the teachers made the first quiz questions really easy. We all knew the right answers, and so everyone remained on the same table and no one had to step down. After a while, however, the three options seemed more and more plausible. For example:

For which one of these three soccer clubs did the legendary Robert "Bobby" Charlton play for most of his career?

Table one: Arsenal

Table two: Manchester United

or

Table three: Liverpool?[28]

Because we weren't allowed to ask each other's advice, we would attempt to look as if we were trying to re-member until someone who seemed likely to know the answer finally picked a table. As soon as three or four or more had joined this person on that table, the rest of us would follow. Everyone chose the same answer, even when we didn't have a clue and all three seemed as likely to be correct.

Sometimes we had reason to assume that someone might know because, judging by appearances, this per-son seemed to have special insight into the subject at hand. For instance, if a cool kid wore a soccer shirt, and the question was on soccer, we would join him in whatever answer he picked. Sometimes he was wrong, but that was okay.

If there was a question about, say, Miss Marple, and someone was wearing cord pants and thick reading glasses—the kind that work like magnifying glasses and turn your eyes into strange fishes in a bowl—this

---

[28] The right answer, in case you care to know, is Manchester United.

might well be the person to follow. There was a guy like that, always with a book under his arm, pretentious and nervous, quoting Shakespeare in a way only he thought amusing. Obviously he was the one bookish enough to know that Agatha Christie was the right answer. But most of us didn't follow him, even if books were the subject. And here is where the assumption about expertise guiding us fails, because it wasn't until the guy in the cool soccer shirt decided to go for the same table as the geeky looking kid that we all decided to stand there too.

In other words, coolness and swagger triumphed over knowledge. What mattered most was not to be right but to be seen with the right people. It was far more preferable to go down with the cool guy than to be remembered as the one who sided with the geek, even though in the end, the latter would prove correct.

There was always an in crowd, a group of people on top of things, and although no one would admit it, we all wished to be part of this group. Thus the game played came to be less and less about trivial knowledge; at the heart of the matter was social hierarchy, and when you are a young teenager, nothing is more important. To be right with the bad-breath-and-uncool-cord-pants guy is to be wrong in a more important sense, even if you're the last ones standing. In this environment, trying to look like you are somehow connected to, or friends with, the soccer shirt rocker is always your safest bet. Forget about the quiz altogether.

So, to the great bemusement of our teachers, the quiz soon turned into a devastating display of teenage group behavior and socio-sexual anxiety. Surviving your teens is not about winning some petty trophy but about being embraced by someone who matters socially. No one wants to be rejected, because rejects, it is presumed, become outcasts for a reason: they are not okay the way they are, because they suck. In our teens, most of us are insecure, and therefore we want to stay close to the person who has the power to reject others. As teenagers we envy, fear, and hate that person, but we want him or her to approve of us so we will not be rejected ourselves.

And so that day, the cooler kid had everyone following in his footsteps. At first, this happened discreetly, but after a while it became more and more obvious. Eventually, our teachers couldn't help but see what was taking place. They had assumed we would want to show what we knew, but we didn't. As our teachers, without realizing it at first, locked knowledge and social status up in a fighting cage, knowledge was going down for the count.

For most of us, this dynamic doesn't change when we grow up. We like to think it does, but it doesn't. It only gets subtler.

You may be one of the exceptions, but if they have the money, most people tend to pay enormous amounts to live in the right neighborhood, even when only a few blocks away they can pay half as much and be just as safe, comfortable, and close to infrastructure.

Westerners throw away pants not because they are worn out but because they don't look cool anymore, and when they don't, those pants have lost their social value. We redecorate our homes not because the wallpaper is torn, the sofa is irreversibly dirty, or the lamp is broken but because the group of people to which we belong—or wish to belong—has moved on to something newer and cooler, and we don't want to look like rejects, left behind on the wrong table.

The process appears irrational, but it's not. If it looks irrational, that means our scope is too narrow and therefore our definition of rationality is inadequate. Humans are herd animals, and we stick to our group because the costs of not doing so are perceived as too high. Back when these behaviors were etched into our DNA, the environment was quite different, and being the reject probably meant your chances of survival turned slim. To the group, carrying the burden of a person guided by unrestrained curiosity was both dangerous and costly.

So if the kid left on the table, insisting on being correct, is not charismatic enough to become our new leader, we will punish his deviant behavior by rejecting him. As grown-ups, we think it is awful when someone is being punished socially. We feel for the reject kid alone on the table and wish to help him, don't we? Some of us will even want to smooth things over by claiming that he hasn't been rejected at all, that it just appears that way. Seeing someone being rejected, some of us will babble about unfortunate circumstances or coincidence, but even if the intention behind such lies is good, they are still lies, and all they do is preserve status quo. We shy away because the image is painful, but that kid indeed is a reject. It is no coincidence, and it might not even be a bad thing, so we shouldn't shy away. Instead, we should take a good look, walk closer, and hail that reject. Heck, why not be that reject?

Some will say none of this applies anymore since these days the nerd has become cool and the geek is now part of the in crowd. But that is not quite the case. Yes, some cool kids and adults pose with nerdy attire to look quirky, but that is not quite the same thing as being a geek. Actually, deliberately posing like one, from a strong social position, is quite the opposite, a demonstration of social strength. In a world that is social through and through, hierarchy is crucial for our future prospects. Therefore, blowing social status by playing the reject is like a rapper in a video dropping hundred-dollar bills through the rolled-down window of his luxury car. It is like saying, "Hey, look, I got so much of this stuff that I can even afford to waste some of it!"

But what about the people we like to call outsiders—people who seem to have nothing to do with the social structure, people who seem to stand beside it or, as the label suggests, outside of it?

The type appeals to many of us because it represents the idea that it is possible to escape from the social hierarchy business, and don't we all sometimes wish to? However, as long as there are at least two humans on this earth, and at some point these two humans interact, social hierarchy will persist. It can shift, and in a healthy companionship you can take turns being on top, but there is no escape from it. You can be temporarily absent from it by living in a cave or on a desert island like Robinson Crusoe, but as soon as Friday shows up, so does social hierarchy.

An outsider is not someone who is outside the hierarchy but someone whose hierarchy membership and status have become blurry because of nonattendance. As soon as the hermit heads back to town, people's behavior toward him will tell us what kind of status he holds.

If we want to create an organization, a family, a company, or a society in which the members are as close to equal as possible, we must first accept the grim dynamics of human interaction. We need to acknowledge that there is a top and a bottom to the social ladder, that we consciously or unconsciously punish each other for trying things that have not been tried before. In fact, it is socially acceptable to achieve almost nothing as long as you do not challenge the values of your group.

If, however, you do not submit to the rules of social behavior, it doesn't matter if you succeed or not. You have offended the values of the group, and you will be punished for doing that. You can avoid retribution only if you are so successful in what you do that you can take on the social norms, establish new values and rules, and become a leader while doing it.

When I was fourteen, anxiously jumping from one table to the next along with the other teenagers, I knew for sure I wasn't ready to do any of these things. I did not want to challenge anything. I just wanted to blend in. I wanted girls to notice me but not at the risk of becoming the reject. Attracting a girl to whom I was attracted seemed too hard, and even though I wanted to do that, I didn't dare step out of the crowd. So when the next quiz question turned out to be about Westminster Palace, I got nervous.

I had watched a TV documentary about the palace just a month earlier, and because my memory is good, I was sure I would know the right answer to the question as long as it was about something that had been mentioned on the show. And that was exactly what happened.

The Other Guy was reading the questions now.

Big Ben in London is famous all over the world, and millions of tourists come to visit Westminster Palace every year. But what exactly does the name Big Ben refer to?

Table one: The bell inside the clock tower

Table two: The large, four-faced clock on the walls of the clock tower

or

Table three: The clock tower itself?

This was a fast one. Everyone decided Big Ben was the clock tower—there wasn't any doubt—and I soon realized I was the only kid who knew Big Ben was in fact the bell.

I cursed my luck. Just knowing the correct answer was enough to make me feel like a total reject. Knowing more than the rest about a thing such as Big Ben now seemed like the uncoolest thing ever, and I faced the worst scenario I could have imagined. No matter how trivial a thing it was to know, just knowing something the others didn't seemed to put me at great risk of becoming a reject.

Everyone, including me, was standing on table three. I knew the correct thing to do was to skip all the way to the table at the other end. I swallowed hard and crossed my fingers, hoping no one was looking at me.

It's the bell. It's the bell, you idiot! a voice inside my head shouted at me, eager to make me move. I struggled hard not to obey the commanding tone of that voice and to swap tables. Part of me felt I owed it to my parents, to the documentary, and to truth in general to jump to the empty table. Remaining where I stood was silly, but the opposition was too strong. Whatever that inner voice was telling me, the rest of me simply refused to listen. In the end, I wasn't even close to leaving the table with everyone else on it. My feet wouldn't move.

I stayed firmly on the wrong table, and so I could watch from a close distance as the Spanish girls and their friends in high heels exchanged giggles and looks of surprise when the Other Guy read out the right answer.

"Actually, Big Ben is the bell inside the clock tower!"

Ta-da.

I studied the Spanish girls. They were outlandishly pretty, but there was also something human about them now, something that very much reminded me of myself, and that's when it came to me.

I watched their eyes, their brows, their mouths, the tilting of their heads, the movement of their hair, the wrinkling of their foreheads, and that was when I got the notion that they too had known all along! I couldn't be sure, but there was something very unconvincing about their gestures. Their looks had seemed like some kind of mutant ability—their beauty was like the strength of the Hulk or the wall climbing skills of Spiderman—and in a way, this had blinded me. I had assumed they could do anything they wanted whenever they felt like it, but now I could see pretense just like mine in their faces. It seemed to me they were on that table for the same reason I was: they too knew this wasn't the right table, and still they stood there! To me, that was the end of it: the quiz, honesty, and a kind of innocence too.

I didn't blame the Spanish girls for being like me, but the charade made everything seem more real and slightly less fantastic. I also saw that this was the reason my parents had sent me abroad to a summer language course in the first place. Sure, correct grammar was a nice bonus, but I realized now that this wasn't the real reason my mom and my stepdad had put me on the plane with a group of strangers and waved good-bye. Their intent was not for me to improve my grammar, to expand my vocabulary, or to acquire a British accent. What they really hoped for was that I would learn important lessons about what it is to be a human being, and guided by that, possibly feel a little less lost in the world.

* * *

In psychoanalytic therapy, there is the concept of bastions.[29] A bastion is an unconscious agreement between the therapist and the patient to keep quiet about something the two feel uncomfortable discussing. This is very bad because it can impede or even stop the progress that is the aim of any therapy. Bastions are not limited to therapy and can be built between any two persons at any time. At times, this is quite necessary. For instance, in Western culture, talking to one's grandparents about their sex life usually is very uncomfortable for both parties. Thus the subject is mutually avoided. In this case, the bastion serves its purpose, but what if you are involved in a project and you have a setback so painful that you turn into a bastion? You're in trouble.

As we started writing this book, we knew we had come up with a brand-new idea. It was fresh and innovative,

---

[29] Madeleine Baranger, Willy Baranger, Jorge Mom, "Process and Non-Process in Analytic Work," *International Journal of Psycho-Analysis* (1983), 64:1–15.

and we would proudly introduce it. The glory of it, the fame! We might even become known as pioneers in management, our own field. We *were* pioneers, we thought—not a bad thing to be at a dinner party when someone asks you what you do for a living. Instead an angry man showed up, convincingly rejecting us and our perspective.

We published a text on the social media networks to share our idea and to see what kind of response we would get. The text we published was roughly the chapter about skepticism, but it didn't include the story of Allan J. McDonald and the rocket launch because we hadn't gotten that far yet. This was a test run, and it included only the more abstract part of the chapter. We didn't see this as extreme, but people were really upset.

We were quite taken aback by the bashing from our prospective readers, especially by the letter from the exceptionally angry man who completely dismissed what we had to say.

The negative reactions—the letter from that man in particular—made us feel like rejects, and this was a painful setback. Our project was grinding to a halt until one day, after a few months had passed, we finally realized that the concept we had found and were in the process of perfecting would show us the way forward. We realized that to become the pioneers we wanted to be—to be groundbreaking in the most positive way—we first had to enter the bastion where we ourselves were the rejects. We needed to be okay with assuming the role of the nerdy teen alone on the table. We needed to dare to step all the way down the social ladder and to accept that some would reject us and what we had to say. When we did this, we could start addressing in a constructive way the negative and sometimes offensive comments we had received.

We sat down with the text again to see what needed to be chiseled out before we could continue. This time, some bits of the text had us laughing. From our newly gained position as rejects, we even toyed with Joakim's home printer, trying to print our texts on toilet paper so we could wipe ourselves with them. We read parts out loud and laughed a lot. "Jeez, that really sucks!" But sometimes we didn't laugh. One of us would say, "Hm ... Read that last part again," and parts of it, we figured, weren't too bad.

We kept reworking the material, growing more serious about it again, and roughly two months later, we pretty much had it figured out, in great part thanks to the angry man. He really did help us! By now, that long, angry letter seemed almost a miracle. It had put us off at first but had eventually showed us the way, and with the writing of the book proceeding nicely, we decided that the least we could do was to thank him. Indeed, we probably would never have stopped to work things through and our idea would have remained half-baked if he had not been so thorough in his critique, so adamant, eloquent, and convincing. Most of all, he had taken the trouble to write us, and so far he had gotten nothing in return.

So we googled his address. It was now our turn to write an honest letter, just like he had done, thanking him for his skeptical critique of our text about the benefits of, well, being a skeptic. We asked if, as an expression of our appreciation for what he had done, we could treat him to lunch or dinner and could talk. We were curious to hear what he thought of our greatly revised text. This was the spirit of the message we put in the mailbox.

We waited, wondering what his response would be. Would he understand how thankful we were? We phoned each other the next day and the day after to see if either of us had received any response, but no, nothing. We worried it might take weeks before we heard from him, but we didn't have to wait long. It took only three days for his response to reach us, and it didn't take us long to read it, as this letter wasn't nearly as lengthy as the first one had been. Except for the date and place at the top of the page and the "Dearest David and Joakim," there was just three words. The second and third were "you both" with quite a few expression marks added, and the first was exactly the kind of rude word our publishing company advised us not to put in a book like this.

By now, we were already rejects, and we were convinced that power could be found in gaining access to the full spectrum between reject and its supposed opposite, pioneer. Now we were moving forward. We had embarked on a pioneering journey together, and our guts were telling us that lots of fun lay ahead. *Suckcess*, we decided, was a good word for it because it seemed to be an expression of the paradox. Nobody on this planet has ever become successful without sucking at times, and that's both fine and necessary. That's the way it must be! We all suck somehow, but whereas before we believed that this ought to keep us from feeling proud of ourselves and reaching our goals, we now decided that practicing the paradox of suckcess was the way forward. We would open the door to the banished parts of ourselves because there, a more real and honest kind of strength was waiting for us to muster the courage to tap it. From now on, we would both suck and be okay with it, and since then, no one has been able to stop us by telling us that we do.

By now, we knew all too well what we had been trying to do before. When we had wanted something badly, we had—mostly without thinking about it—started to fear the opposite. When we had set a goal for ourselves, we would do everything in our power to ignore the opposite of that goal. Once we had set our sights on success of any kind, a quiet and unaddressed fear of failure would build up inside of us and between us, and both of us would do our best never to mention it. If we wanted to win, losing was the much-feared opposite of our goal; if we dedicated ourselves to going all the way to the finish, we did just about anything not to be quitters. The more we wanted to reach our goal, the tighter the grip of the opposite would become, until trying to reach our goal became scary, painful, and even impossible.

By now, what the angry man represents for us is the fear of becoming a reject when you set out to become a pioneer. The way to move ahead is to deliberately stop, to hear out that angry man, and to accept that a reject and a pioneer are just different sides of the same coin. We learned that to become a pioneer, you must first access your inner reject. You need both. Instead of running away, the thing to do is to pay serious attention to what that person so eager to reject you has to say, to take that much-feared position, and to sit down right next to him. Make yourself comfortable in his company, spend so much time with him that when you are done, *he* will be the one who cannot stand *you* anymore! Scrutinize his perspective, invite him, and beg for more until he tells you to fuck off.

CONCLUSION

We have put forth our case. We have done so by telling seven disparate real-life stories, which have in common that thing we call the paradox of suckcess.

If you are the CEO of a corporation manufacturing cars, and you strive to be as flawless as a saint in your doings, you better admit to the fact that you are a sinner, or your sins will keep you and the people around you from reaching your goal.

If you are a pirate fighting to go all the way to the finish, the ability to quit in the midst of anything you do will get you there.

If you are a coach facing the strongest opposition your sport has ever seen and you still want to win, mastering being a loser will prove necessary.

If you are a loving parent eager to be the hero who comes to the rescue of your child, you can fill that role by accepting that you are also the victim of circumstances that you will never be able to fully control.

If you are a scientist who wants to reach the glory of a genius, you cannot let fear of looking like a fool hold you back.

If you are an engineer eager to create a space rocket that is possible only if you believe, you better make sure you are not held hostage by an organization that fears skepticism.

If you are a regular teen yearning to do what for someone of your years is the act of a pioneer, then slowly but surely acquire the courage to take the position of the reject.

For now, that's all we have to say. We hope it was meaningful, thought-provoking, and helpful to you.

ABOUT THE AUTHORS

Joakim Ahlström is an internationally recognized expert and pioneer in the field of leadership and personal development. His ability to harness human potential and inspire high performance has contributed to the success of global companies such as Coca-Cola, Volvo, Ericsson, and IKEA.

AHLSTRÖM **&**
HIRASAWA

David Hirasawa is a practical thought leader who works with management, strategy, and leadership development at an international company. He has a background in political theory and philosophy, and his ability to bring stories to life has made him a highly appreciated author within the popular literature genre.

Lightning Source UK Ltd.
Milton Keynes UK
UKOW04f1113300118
317064UK00002B/23/P